SIMON

WRITE

FOR

INFLUENCE

maximize the effectiveness of your writing

Coombe
Hill
Publishing

Published by Coombe Hill Publishing
33 Melrose Gardens
New Malden
Surrey KT3 3HQ
United Kingdom

coombehillpublishing.com

Background image on cover: © saicle/123RF Stock Photo

ISBN: 9781910398203 (paperback)
ISBN: 9781910398210 (ePub)

A big thank you to Cathleen Small for her editorial input.

7 May 2018

Table of Contents

Chapter 4
Vocabulary: The Words You Write   51

A Matter of Approach

W e commit words to the page for a reason. Typically, we write to transmit information and we transmit information with the purpose of influencing.

That influence may be to help the reader to learn a new fact.

That influence may be to encourage the reader to consider a different perspective and maybe revisit their opinions.

We write with the intent of bringing about a change in another person; no one writes without intending some effect. And if you're intending to influence, then you will want to maximize the effectiveness of your words.

Whether you are writing a short web post, a letter, an essay, a report, a thesis, an entire book, or anything in between, this book is your companion and guide to a deliberate and methodical approach to writing in order to maximize the authority and power of that written message.

No Rules, Just Principles

Anyone can type, but typing isn't the same as writing. Writing isn't the same as communicating, and communicating is not equivalent to influencing. There may be a continuum—from typing to influence—but one does not automatically follow the other.

Publishing—the process of making text available for other people to consume—is open to everyone. People publish, in some cases many times daily, for personal and for business-related reasons. Some publishing goes wide (for instance, a post on a social media site) and some is for a very specific, tightly controlled audience (as is often the case with business-related matters, where there is usually a confidential aspect).

The potential outlets for publishing are numerous— social media, websites, blogs, news sites, brochures, books, business proposals, and reports to list a few—and people consume text in a variety of ways, including from printed material, on computer screens, or with a snatched glance at a smartphone.

Reaching the end goal (influence) from the starting point of the written word is a matter of approach and application of principles. Each logical step needs to be followed, and missing a step doesn't simply degrade the result, but potentially stops the effectiveness completely.

The aim of this book is to challenge you and to provide a structure you can use to think about your writing. You can then make up your own mind about the appropriate principles to apply for any specific piece of writing in any specific situation.

Why Does Text Matter?

In a world where we are bombarded with sounds and images, where photographs are shared as soon as they're shot, and where everybody can make and share a video just using their phone, many people wonder why text has any relevance.

In short, text remains relevant because text remains relevant. That might sound quite glib (and it is quite glib), but text remains relevant because it has many advantages as a medium for communication and therefore for influence. Let's look some of those advantages.

- Text is ubiquitous. It can be read on any screen. There's no need for a special player or a plug-in. There's no need for a minimum screen size in order to see the detail. And indeed, with paper-based documents there's no need for any further technology to consume the text (unless the reader requires glasses).

- Text is scannable. The reader can cast their eye over the material to preview what they are about to read. When consuming text, the reader can pause, reflect, maybe reread a line or two, and then continue. Equally, if the reader wants, they can flick back to an earlier section to check a detail and then continue to read.

- Elements of a text document can be highlighted and extracted. So, for instance, it is easy to select a small quote from text and send that quote on.

- The file size of text documents is tiny (especially when compared to audio or video files). A small file size makes storage and distribution far more practical.

- Text is searchable, both within an individual piece and more generally. So, for instance, a document can be searched for on a computer or found through one of the internet search engines. While the technology for image-based search is improving every day, it is still nowhere near the quality and does not offer the precision of text search.

When we write, we need to understand the medium and be cognizant of how our readers—the people we are trying to influence—will be consuming that writing. Writing has many advantages over other media, and by optimizing the output for the medium we can apply those advantages to increase our influence.

Laying the Foundation

There is no one simple: *this is what you must do to influence with your writing.* Instead, there are many small elements that must all be brought together and into alignment.

The structure of the writing—how those many small elements are presented to the reader—matters since this is the journey on which the reader will be taken. But the approach of the writer—how the writer thinks about the writing before starting to write—also matters because it has such a direct effect on the text. Equally, much of writing is about what is not written. Half of the battle is removing what is not needed and cutting out any distractions.

Writing has little to do with putting the words down—it's how you think about the writing before you write, how you approach the writing, how you structure the writing, and how you review the material after you've finished writing and before it is published.

With that in mind, let's move on and think about who will be reading what you write.

Chapter 1

Who: Thinking About the Reader

E very piece of writing needs a reader. Before you start writing, you first need to determine who your reader is. If there is no reader, then who are you influencing?

Who Is Your Reader?

Until you have a firm grasp on the identity or the nature of your reader, you can't begin to craft the words and marshal the facts to create a message that will resonate. This isn't an issue you can skip: you would talk with a five-year-old in a very different manner from how you would talk with a fifty-year-old.

The content of your writing cannot have relevance until there is context for what you are trying to say. But trying to understand who the reader actually is, is not always straightforward.

Specificity of the Reader

Often you will want to influence one specific person, quite often someone you know and have interacted with in person. This may be a client you are advising or a person whose opinion you disagree with and who you want to influence to consider another course. Whatever the situation, you will be able to clearly identify one person to whom your message is directed.

This is the most straightforward situation because you will be focusing your content on one person.

Generality of the Reader

At other times, your audience will be wider than one person. For instance, in writing this book, I intend for more than one person to read it.

When writing for a broader audience, the key issue is to focus. If the writing is directed at a potential audience of everybody in the world plus all sentient aliens in the known universe, then its relevance is likely to be highly blunted because the concepts will have to account for all and any potential readers.

When there is a generality of readers, it is helpful to focus on categories and individuals who may be representative of a wider group. So, for instance, if you are writing an article about selecting schools, the audience could be generalized to parents. While other people may have an interest in your subject, writing with parents in mind will provide a focus.

And note, I say *a* focus, not the *only* focus. Not all parents will be interested, and there will be other people who may not be parents who may have an interest. But before you can start writing, you need to narrow down your potential audience from *everybody in the known universe* to something closer to *all potential readers*.

Primary Readers, Secondary Readers

It is unlikely that anything of any merit will be read by only one person (your primary reader), even if the content is given in confidence to one person. If the content has any merit—if the ideas influence one person and that person then wants to pass on the information to others—then the writing will be shared with these secondary readers.

Equally, you may be in a situation where you prepare a piece of text for one person, but you know that others will see the content. The primary reader may be an executive in a business charged with looking after one area, but the secondary readers may have overlapping interests (for instance, they may be representatives from finance or human resources).

When writing, you should be aware of these secondary readers. The knowledge that there may be secondary readers shouldn't change the content, but you might want to consider the details, the context, and the language you employ.

Identifying the Right Audience, Not Simply the Loudest Voice

When there's a loud voice it can be tough to focus on the identity of the actual reader.

For instance, if your boss has asked you to write some words for a client, it's easy to think the reader is your boss. This is wrong—the reader is the client. In this example, your boss may be a secondary reader, but the primary reader—the person who should be foremost in your attention—is your client.

The secondary readership is never unimportant, but the primary audience is always more significant.

As well as your primary reader and secondary readers, also be aware that you may have readers who are not your audience. Particularly when you publish in public forums, you can find many people offering their comments—and not always favorable comments. As long as you've fully understood who your readers are, then you can feel confident in ignoring anyone who is not your audience—these were the people you never set out to influence in the first place.

If they're not your intended readers, then these are not the people you are seeking to influence, and these people will not be changed by your words. Ignore them and don't waste your time trying to make people happy whom you can never satisfy.

Communicate

Once you know who your reader is—in other words, you know who you are directing your writing to—then you can think about communicating with them. With the identity of the reader, you're no longer writing generically, you're communicating with a specific person (or group of people).

The Basics of Communication

Communication is not about what you, the writer, say (or write). Communication is what the reader understands.

Read that first paragraph again—it's perhaps the most important paragraph in this book.

What you write doesn't matter. What the reader thinks you wrote is all that is relevant. The reader's interpretation is the definitive interpretation of your text. So when you write, write within a frame of reference that the reader will understand.

Now read that first paragraph again; it really is that important. In fact, go further: scribble it on a piece of paper and stick it on the wall.

Communicating with the Reader

If you cannot communicate, you cannot influence. It's that simple.

If you cannot communicate with your intended reader, then you cannot influence your intended reader.

This might seem very rudimentary—and it is—but it is fundamental. When you put down words, what you think is irrelevant. All that matters is what the reader—the specific reader you have identified—understands from those words. That understanding is on the reader's terms, not yours. Your intentions in communicating are irrelevant, and there are no second chances once you have committed to your words.

The reader should be able to read something once and understand exactly what you want them to understand. They should be able to understand because it is written in terms that mean something to them. If the reader has to first understand you, the writer, and the perspective you're bringing, then the communication will be degraded.

The communication will be degraded because the reader—assuming they continue to read—will be focused on trying to understand and parse what you meant. In other words, the reader won't be focusing on the message you have tried (and failed) to convey.

In short, if the reader isn't going to be able to understand what you write, then you will not be communicating, and if you're not communicating, then don't bother with the writing and publishing in the first place.

Understand the Reader's Perspective

When you seek to communicate with a reader, you are communicating with a human being.

Human beings are very imperfect beasts, and while we mostly live our lives with good intentions, we sometimes fail. As writers, we need to be sensitive to the challenges a reader may have and write in a way that minimizes the impact of outside forces in the reader's life that may lead to our message not being read.

Clearly, if the intention of writing is to have influence, then you need to actually be read, and if you're going to hope to be read, then you need to consider what might stop the potential reader from actually reading your piece.

Interest

The first question you need to ask yourself is whether the content of your writing is of interest to your reader.

The content may be of interest to you. The content may be very important, for you. But that interest, that importance, does not make the issue interesting or important for the reader.

If you cannot answer the simple question of what makes the topic important for your intended reader, then do not start writing.

Benefit to the Reader

It's not enough to simply be interesting (as in, here's an interesting fact you may not know...). Instead, the information needs to be interesting and actionable—in other words, the reader must be able to do something with the information you are giving them.

The reader must be able to clearly see a link between what you have written and an action on their part, which then provides a benefit to the reader. Let's step through that slowly:

- In reading what you have written, the reader must be able to understand—on their terms—what you are saying.

- On the basis of what you have said, the reader must be able to see what action they personally can take in order to effect a change.

- The reader must be able to understand the benefit to themselves of that change.

Get those steps right, and you'll have the reader's interest.

Time and Distractions

There are twenty-four hours in any day. Your reader will allocate those twenty-four hours according to their priorities, not yours. Just because you have time within your twenty-four hours, that doesn't mean the reader does.

Your reader will read your piece at a time that suits them.

If you have focused on providing content that is interesting *for the reader* and that offers benefit *for the reader*, then you will greatly increase the chances of your piece being read. If there is little to interest the reader, then the chance of the writing reaching the top of the list of priorities is slim, and if it does, then the reader is liable to be distracted.

Limits and Disengagement

Even when you get to the point that your reader reads your entire piece, they may not engage. If you are seeking to influence, then your piece will require some intellectual engagement by the reader—in short, you will want them to think and perhaps to challenge their own beliefs.

Most people have a finite limit to the number of fights they can have in any one day (including fights with themselves). Most people have a finite limit to the number of decisions they can make in any one day.

Even with the very best writing, if the reader has reached their limit for that day, then they will mentally disengage.

Outcome

So now you understand your reader and you understand your reader's perspective. That means you're ready, right?

Not quite.

Let's think about what you are expecting from the communication.

What Do You Want to Change?

If you are writing with the intention of influencing, then you are expecting—or at least hoping for—some change. There are two main sides to these changes.

The first side is what you want for yourself from the communication. If you're writing with the intention of influencing, then there must be some benefit for you. You must be expecting some change in your world.

The second side is the reaction you are expecting from the reader. You are presenting the reader with information—how do you expect the reader to react when they have consumed that new knowledge? Now take this thought further: what measurable reaction are you expecting? If you're not expecting a reaction—if you're not expecting an outcome that is measurable in some manner—then what is the purpose of your communication? What influence do you expect to have?

It is perfectly acceptable—legally, morally, ethically, or however you view an issue—to seek to influence someone in order to acquire a personal benefit. However, when thinking how to write where the aim is influence, you need to be aware of where the center of gravity lies.

I'll return to this thought in a moment, but first, let's consider how the reader may be influenced.

How Are You Trying to Influence?

Simplistically, humans react to two motivators: fear and greed. These are crude and fairly ugly terms, but in a broad sense they are descriptive.

Fear

Fear—particularly, fear of loss—is the more significant of fear and greed.

As humans, we fear losing what we have. We fear losing our money/source of income, our homes, our family, and our friends. We fear losing face/prestige and losing influence. We fear for our safety and we fear—at one remove—for the safety of our families and our friends.

If we have "it," if we enjoy or appreciate "it," then we have a fear of losing it.

Greed

Greed is the secondary motivator. Secondary because generally (but not always) humans are more driven by fear of loss than they are by possible gain. There's a certain logic here—humans are more concerned with actual loss than potential gain.

We are greedy for gain and will seek to gain money, material, power, influence, and reputation. And of course, if we have lost, then we will seek to regain.

Let me give a simple example of fear and greed in practice. Parenting is all about fear and greed. Parents are fearful for their children (will they get hurt, will they suffer detriment, and so on) while at the same time being greedy for their children (they want them to have every advantage possible). As you can understand from this example, fear and greed are not ignoble motivators, but they can have a powerful effect on behavior. Spend a few moments looking around and try to figure why anyone does what they do—if you can't link what has happened to fear or greed, you're probably not thinking hard enough.

Using the terms fear and greed are useful for illustration, but we can take a gentler approach. When seeking to influence—and making the case for the reader—you need to focus on:

- The potential detriment—this is the fear angle.

- The potential gain—this is the greed angle.

When you can link your influence to avoiding a detriment or to a possible gain for your reader, then you have found a lever for influence. If you're not making a connection to either a gain or a detriment for the reader, then you'll probably find it difficult to craft a message that will interest the reader.

Linking Motivation with Context

A moment ago, we looked at the potential beneficiaries from any changes that you are seeking to catalyze and saw that there are two very different conversations to be had:

- On one side, we're asking solely for our own benefit.

- On the other side, we're presenting the reader with a situation in which we both benefit.

If there's no benefit for the reader, then we're just begging. However, if there is a benefit for the reader, then we're working toward mutual self-interest. Both approaches are valid, but the nature of the conversation affects how we try to influence.

Begging

I'm using an ugly word again: begging. And the reason I'm using an ugly word is because there is never a happy story that goes with a situation in which we are seeking to influence only for ourselves (or those close to us).

In a situation where you are asking solely for yourself with no motivation for the reader to help—in other words, no realistic opportunities to play on the reader's fear or greed—then the scope to influence is severely restricted.

If you truly have no leverage, then the only realistic approach is to highlight the human aspect and hope to make an emotional connection that overrides the reader's rational response.

Win/Win

Trying to influence someone to take an action, when that action is in their best interest, can be a straightforward proposition.

The benefit to the reader may be an avoidance of loss or may be the accrual of a benefit, but in either case (or both cases—it's possible to avoid and gain simultaneously) there's no need to actively seek to persuade. For the writer, it's more a case of giving the reader the basic facts—with a nod toward the fear and greed motivators—such that the reader can reach the conclusion on their own.

Ethically you'll likely want to disclose your own self-interest, but so much of the influencing is just getting out of the way. If there's a clear case to be made, then it's for you to lose, not one that requires a huge amount of negotiating talent or persuasion skills.

Now, clearly, in the real world there are very few instances where there is a benefit to be had that is cost and consequence free. And usually, if there is a benefit to be had without any downside, then the person who can benefit will have already taken advantage, so your scope for influence will be limited.

However, the far more frequent situation is one where there is a benefit, but also a consequence. For example, if

someone wants to buy a house, there may be clear benefits—
it gives them somewhere to live, it offers security, and it may
be a great investment. But there is a consequence—a house
will cost money, and the potential purchaser may not have
the money or may want to spend their money in another
manner.

In a situation where there is a benefit, but also a
consequence to that benefit, the key levers to influence are
fear and greed.

Reframing Begging as a Win/Win

We've looked at the situation where there is benefit to
you, the writer, but no benefit to the reader. In this case,
you're effectively left to beg, perhaps highlighting the human
aspect in the hope of eliciting an emotional response.

There is an alternative approach to begging: reconsider
your proposition and reframe it to include a benefit for the
reader. What do I mean by reframing? In short:

- Express the proposition in a different manner.

- Look at the situation from a different angle.

- Find a different context for the issue.

The point is not simply to change your words and still
end up with the same answer. Instead, change something
in what you are seeking and look for a way that you can
link what you want with a benefit for the reader. Look to
the reader's fear and greed and find a place where there is
common interest.

Once you have that intersection of common interest,
work from there.

Take care to avoid reaching and making an extreme or
unnecessary construction in order to make your argument.
Don't present an obscure or imprecise benefit that relies on
many factors that neither you nor the reader can control.

Equally, avoid false imperatives. For instance, don't
suggest that you will write to the newspapers and create

public relations problems for the reader if they don't yield to your requests. That is straightforward blackmail.

You may not be able to find a mutually beneficially position, and if you can't, that's acceptable. And if you can't find a way to make that link, consider why you're approaching this person. Not everyone can be influenced.

Is Your Outcome Realistic?

Realistic is an interesting word. The nature of realism is highly subjective, and any view about whether an outcome is realistic will be colored by personal concerns.

Perhaps an easier way to consider whether your outcome is realistic is to look at the practical objectives to achieving the outcome. In this case, we're back to fear and greed. If you want to influence a change, then look at who will lose through that change. Focus on any fear—real or imagined. But also, focus on greed—if you've seen a benefit, then others will have seen a benefit and they'll want that gain for themselves.

Anything and everything is achievable; the only real questions are how and over what period.

Only you can decide what timescale is acceptable. As for the how... The most straightforward approach is to break down any goal into smaller chunks—look for smaller achievements that, taken together, will lead to the outcome you want. This approach has several advantages:

- It moves you past an all-or-nothing approach. Instead, you can accumulate small wins.

- Accumulating small wins allows you to build momentum and set the direction of travel in your ongoing influencing.

- As you improve your written influence skills, you can influence in more strategically important areas.

- You can build a relationship with the person or people you're trying to influence. Influence is far more effective when it is wielded by a trusted partner.

What If I Disagree with the Reader?

Very often you will want to influence a reader because you disagree with their opinion. That may be a comparatively trivial disagreement, or it may be a disagreement over something that you regard as being an absolutely fundamental matter of principle.

So how do you approach someone who has opinions that you find offensive—perhaps grossly offensive?

Before we go further, it is important to understand the limitation of the written word, especially if you are dealing with a time-limited issue. If you believe someone is trying to exterminate you and all your people, then a written attempt to influence may not be the best form of protection, especially if the threat is imminent.

Assuming there is no imminent threat, start with understanding.

First, Seek to Understand

Before you can seek to influence, you need to understand the other person.

If someone has the same knowledge as you, the same values as you, the same life experience as you, and the same perspective as you, then it is likely they would share your opinions (and therefore little influence will be necessary). When someone holds a different view, it is not simply a matter of that other person being irrational or wrong—it is a matter that different life experiences have shaped their views.

So, step one is to try to understand what in the other person's experience leads to the view with which you disagree.

Very often opinions will be wrapped up in matters of identity or founded on (what appear from the outside to be) irrational beliefs that support very primal fears. (See, it all comes back to fear and greed.)

On the flip side, your views will be wrapped up in your identity and may be founded on irrational beliefs. This isn't to suggest that your views are wrong or misguided—simply that the route by which you reached the views you are seeking to expound may be questionable. It is this questionable route to settling your views that may, in part, make it harder for you to find a way into understanding the other person's perspective.

In short, don't start with a preconceived notion—simply focus on the other person and how they reached their view.

Empathy, Compassion

Once you have an understanding of the factors driving the other person's view—and you understand how those motivations differ from yours—then approach the person with empathy and compassion. Even if you disagree, treat the other person with respect.

No one is simply evil or wrong; there is a reason behind every attitude. You can't start to influence unless you understand.

As a side note, I say no one is evil. Clearly, some people are—for instance, some people are psychopaths. In these cases, I'm not sure there is any merit to seeking to influence with words, since these people are unlikely to be swayed by reason. By equal measure, anyone with whom you have a disagreement is not automatically a psychopath.

Once you understand, then you can begin to craft your argument in terms that are relevant to the reader. There's no point in putting forward a summary of your perspective—explain the issue in terms that matter to the reader. You're not going to influence by shouting—you need to find a way to explain in terms that matter to your reader.

The Wrangle

At this point, I suspect you're thinking, "I want to say *this*, my prime reader wants to hear *that*, and the secondary reader will think something else completely." And you're probably right—you're dealing with at least three potentially differing opinions.

So how do you square the circle?

First, ignore those whom you're not trying to directly influence. Look to your primary reader and be aware of your secondary reader. Ignore anyone who is not in those categories.

As I've said several times, find the reader's perspective and write in their terms. Find the common ground, build a relationship, and then build from there.

You won't simply make a social media post and change the world. But if you take the time to build a relationship founded on trust and respect, then over time, you will have influence.

Can't I Just Get Writing?

Why does this all matter...can't I just get writing? I know what I want to say and you're just making me think about stuff I don't care about.

Thinking about the reader matters because we're writing with an end goal: influence. We're not trying to be entertaining or come up with clever, beautiful words; we're trying to effect change. To effect change, we need to focus on exactly what change we want from exactly whom.

Once we've identified the reader and we understand their motivations and the benefit of what we have to say for the reader, then we can begin to communicate with them. To begin to communicate, we need to structure our argument and present the right information in the right order.

Chapter 2

How: Structure

When we write for influence, we need to provide the right words, in the right order. The aim is to convey the message—while using the levers of influence—with maximum efficiency.

Any minor block can lead to our words being tossed aside or ignored. The text should be immediately comprehensible—the reader should understand on the first reading. If the reader needs to work to understand what you're saying, or if the reader misinterprets what you're saying, then you're lost.

But we're in luck. When it comes to crafting our words, we have a lot of context to help us frame the message:

- We know our primary reader and our secondary readers.

- We know that the aim in writing is to influence our readers. We are influencing, not entertaining.

- We know that we're providing text and that text has advantages (for instance, the reader can preview, review, scan, and skip over whole chunks).

With that context, let's move on to thinking about the structure.

Capture, Engage, Influence

It would be wrong to equate putting down words with influencing.

There is a link, but there is also a process by which one leads to the other. As writers, we need to take the reader on a journey, and there are several key staging posts on that journey:

■ Attract attention

■ Hold attention

■ Communicate

One follows the other, and you cannot do one without having done the previous. Let's look at these steps in a bit more detail.

Attract Attention

I hope it's self-evident that if you don't attract your potential reader's attention, then your potential reader won't become an actual reader, and without a reader, you have no opportunity to influence.

If you have many potential primary readers, then you need to attract the attention of each and every one of those potential readers. If your words are going to be read by secondary readers, then you need to attract the attention of each and every one of those secondary readers. If your writing is going to be shared more widely beyond your target groups, then you need to attract the attention of all of those potential readers.

No attention means no opportunity to influence. It doesn't mean a degraded chance or degraded influence—it means zero chance to influence and zero change.

Starting to Attract Attention

The first step to attracting attention is to look to the potential primary reader. Look to their interest.

Ignore what you want to say; start with what the reader wants to hear. Clearly, if you don't know who your potential reader is, then you won't know what will engage them.

Clickbait

If you've spent any time online, then you'll know about clickbait—links to entice you to click. They're usually salacious or overblown—you won't believe!!!!—or they hint at celebrities and sex, but they're almost always disappointing and leave the reader dissatisfied.

So why do websites engage in this practice?

In short, because it works. It drives traffic to their site, and that traffic generates advertising revenue. The difficulty, however, is that it may work once or twice, but it is not sustaining since it is essentially a technique based on trickery.

If you write for influence, you will find that clickbait-style wording works in attracting attention.

However, like clickbait, there is a downside. Clickbait uses trickery to fool readers, and when readers know they've been fooled generally that's the point at which they stop reading. If you fool your potential readers, they're going to stop reading and they're not going to share your writing. Added to which, you'll have made the potential reader feel ashamed, and if you make them feel shame, then they're never going to respect you or your opinions.

If your reader stops reading, then the opportunity to influence is gone.

If you have made your potential reader feel foolish, then they're not going to share your words.

Attract attention through understanding your potential reader's interest and giving them something that hooks into that interest.

Remember the Reader

As you attract attention, as you try to hold the reader's attention, remember the reader.

Readers have better things to do than read rubbish. Time is finite—each day has only twenty-four hours, and even the fastest reader can consume only a finite amount of content within those twenty-four hours. The way that most readers manage this issue is not to read, or to stop reading.

It doesn't matter how important you are. It doesn't matter how significant your topic is. If a reader perceives that reading your text is a waste of their time, they will not read it. To repeat: this is about the reader, not about you. You do not know what matters in the reader's world; therefore, you need to make what you write as easy to consume as possible in order to help your reader. It's a basic courtesy.

Hold Attention

Once you've got your reader's attention, then you need to keep that attention. If you lose that attention—if the reader stops reading—then any chance of influence stops.

You need to keep your reader's attention from the beginning until the end. It is a constant process. If you lose your reader on page five out of one hundred, then you're not losing the reader for one page—you're losing your reader, end of story. The reader will not read page five, page six, or page seven. The reader will not read any of the other pages. Once the reader stops reading, they're gone.

And the way to hold the reader's attention? Don't be boring. Seriously, don't bore your reader. Keep on the topic and focus on the benefits to the reader. Every page, every paragraph, ruthlessly focus on what you're telling the reader.

Remember, the moment at which you lose attention is the moment at which your influence ceases.

Communicate

Communication is not about what the writer says. Communication is what the reader understands.

You've seen that paragraph before, and I'm repeating it because it's important.

Once you have the reader's attention, then you can communicate. Only when you communicate can you influence. If you stop communicating—if you start thinking in terms of what you want to say rather than focusing on what the reader understands—then you stop influencing.

Structure

Any piece of writing requires structure. Structure so that the reader can understand what is being communicated. Structure to give the writing context. Structure to lead the reader through a process such that the issue can be understood and the influence becomes compelling.

With this structure, remember the basic steps:

- Attract attention

- Hold attention

- Communicate

TL;DR

If you're writing a longer piece—longer is usually understood by the context, but if you're unsure, work on the notion that anything over three hundred words is long—then start with a summary. This may be labeled however you want—TL;DR (too long; didn't read), summary, executive summary (because it's for important people, right?)—or it may be an unlabeled first sentence, but its function is the same: to highlight the key points.

Of course, these are not your key points, these are the key points that matter to your reader. Even in summary, you need to attract and hold attention and then communicate, if you are to have influence.

One aspect of adding a summary is that you increase the likelihood that people will read *only* the summary. You can't stop this—but what you can do is ensure that your summary conveys your influence in its most distilled form.

Brevity

The aim should be to say what is necessary in the fewest words.

You need to add enough words to ensure your reader fully understands what you are saying, but no more. Any additional words represent a waste of time for your reader. If you are happy to waste your reader's time, then clearly you do not respect your reader. If you do not respect your reader, then this will likely have an effect on your ability to influence.

Equally, if you are happy to waste someone else's time, that says something about you—something not very complimentary.

An argument is not stronger because it is longer. On the contrary, if you can't make your argument shorter, then you probably don't fully grasp the important issues you are trying (but actually failing) to communicate.

There is no correlation between length and significance. The United States Declaration of Independence has fewer than 1,500 words—time would suggest it has served its purpose well and that its brevity is, and remains, a strength.

If you are not brief, if you become uninteresting, then you're going to lose attention.

And to repeat myself (again, and yes, the irony of using more words in a section headed "Brevity" isn't lost on me), it doesn't matter how important your message is. If you have lost attention, then you have lost the chance to influence.

To Start

Start with something that interests your reader.

Don't begin with the background. Don't explain how this is a report and recount who hired you. Don't begin with the aims of the document. Don't explain how you were playing with your kids and one asked an interesting question…. Begin with something that directly and immediately interests the reader.

When you start with something that interests the reader, you will attract their attention.

If you start with something that interests you or that gives deep background to a point you intend to make in twenty pages, then you will bore—and therefore lose—your reader.

Start with the end. Start with what you're saying. Start with the answer. And then only include sufficient context as is necessary for the reader to understand what you're saying.

Let me give you an example. Say you're writing a piece about healthy living in order to lose weight. In simplistic terms (and I'm being very simplistic to illustrate my point), the conclusion of your piece may be: eat less and exercise more.

You could make that your first line.

However, that line lacks context and lacks specificity. It's also quite an aggressive approach, commanding everyone. While I'm not against taking a straightforward approach— indeed, I endorse such writing—it's simply not clear *who* this conclusion is aimed at. *For the reader*, it's not clear why this conclusion would interest them.

But if you add some context, then it changes the shape of the message: if you want to lose weight—and maintain a healthy weight—eat less and exercise more.

In this example, I've added enough context to explain the conclusion, but it's also context to hook the reader's interest. A reader can immediately make the direct link between the words and their self-interest.

Context and Background

So, you start with *the answer*, but what about all this spare context you've got lying around? Am I suggesting you hit the delete key?

No.

There is a time and a place for context and background. That time and place is immediately before the information that is supported by the context. In other words, don't give the context on page one and the conclusion on page five hundred. Instead, put the context with the conclusion on page five hundred.

If you've got details and additional information, then add those details immediately before they are *necessary*. Giving background that has no application leaves the reader wondering: Why do I care? As soon as the reader realizes they don't care about something, then it's a small leap for them not to care about anything you're writing. And once the reader doesn't care, influence ends.

Adding context and background—and the right context and background—is as much art as science. Too much background and you will bore and therefore lose the reader. Too little background and you'll lose the context, making what you're trying to say incomprehensible, again with the result of losing the reader.

As the writer, you need the goldilocks approach to background. If you're unsure whether the background is necessary—and it must be necessary, not simply desirable on your part to be said—then delete the background. Having deleted the background, has the comprehension changed? Is the comprehension better because you've simplified your point? Or is comprehension worse because the context is lost? Only you can make this call.

Action

Perhaps the most disappointing question you'll ever hear from a reader is: What am I meant to do with this?

As an aside, you won't hear the question. The reader will silently voice it to themselves as they put your words aside and move on.

The reason this is the most disappointing question is that you have both succeeded and failed. You have succeeded in engaging and communicating with a reader, but you have failed in your influence.

Influence is about persuading others to take action. If you do not explain the action you want your reader to take—and explain it in terms that the reader understands—then you have failed. If the action is ambiguous, contradictory, or in any way not obvious to implement—and implement quickly—then you have failed.

The failure may come for many reasons; for instance, the reader may get bored before they get to the relevant text, or the reader may simply not understand what you're saying. The reason doesn't matter, the failure does.

Headings

In many ways, headings are invisible to the reader. The reader knows the headings are there—there's a different font and a bit of space—but the reader doesn't bother reading the headings. And many legal documents explicitly state that the headings don't affect the interpretation of the text.

So why bother with headings?

Because they matter.

They are invisible...except when they're not. And when they're not invisible, they're highly significant. While we, as readers, may instinctively and involuntarily skip headings, we only do that because, as readers, we're so accustomed to headings and we understand their function at an innate level.

Headings for Readers

Headings provide many benefits for readers.

First, they provide an obvious outline, mapping out the route through the writer's thought process. The headings demonstrate to the reader that there is form and structure—there is a path to follow.

Beyond a simple outline, headings provide a way for readers to scan what is to come.

Readers can scan forward and back, perhaps looking to check a detail. And when they later review the text, readers can scan the heading with some understanding of what each section contains.

Headings also provide a convenient place for readers to pause and contemplate with the certainty that they've reached the end of a thought and it will not be contradicted in the next sentence.

Headings for Writers

For writers, headings offer a way to outline our thoughts and to provide a superior—being immediate and explanatory—table of contents. They offer a chance to telegraph intent to the reader, and with running heads at the top of physical pages (as with the print edition of this book) they give a constant nudge to the reader, reminding of the direction of travel.

Headings also offer the reader a chance to focus. Each heading provides a new and discrete chunk of thought that can be perfectly polished for the reader's consumption.

Headings, Subheadings, Sub-Subheadings

Two questions often arise with headings:

- How many headings do I need?

- How many levels of headings should there be?

While somewhat trite, the answer is simple: as many as there need to be, and no more.

The key purpose of headings is to guide a reader through your text. Every signpost on the journey gives the reader context. However, at a certain point, too many markers just get in the way and start causing confusion.

A heading should also provide a logical grouping. It shouldn't be a break just because a section feels a bit long. As an aside, if a section *feels* long, it probably *is* long, and the appropriate response here is to cut some unnecessary text.

If a section is long, you should also look to subheadings to break up a longer whole into smaller logical chunks. As with headings, subheadings are not added *just because*, but in order to indicate that the following piece of text is a discrete chunk of information.

Sub-subheadings can be useful, but as a general rule, if you're routinely getting to that level of granularity, there's something bigger wrong with the structure of your writing.

As with all writing, with a firm understanding of your primary reader, you will be able to make the best choices for headings, subheadings, and sub-subheadings. Just ask yourself what will best help your reader.

Length

If you can say what you need to say in three hundred words, then say it in three hundred words. There is no benefit to the writer or the reader in using more words than necessary. Longer doesn't increase your chance of influence—in fact, there's generally an indirect correlation between length and influence achieved.

However, if you do need to write more than a few words, then do. There will be times when you need to write a large number of words—this book is an example of a topic where I couldn't say everything I needed to say in three hundred words or even in five thousand words.

To repeat: say what you need to say in the fewest words, but if you *need* to write more, then write more. Note: write more if you *need* to write more, not if you can't be bothered to edit your work shorter or you don't know how to express yourself clearly in a few words or you're just a bad writer.

There are consequences for writing longer. One consequence is that by writing longer, you will need to further extend the piece to bring in more context so your reader can understand the point you are making without needing to follow a spider's web of cross-references. For instance, if you bring up a concept in chapter one, then return to the topic in chapter three, you will need to summarize the concept in chapter three to give your reader context.

Another consequence is that readers will not be able to consume your entire piece in one sitting. Obviously, the more words you write, the longer it will take to read the writing, but also, the more chance that there will be a break in between reading sessions. And once readers take a break, then the period over which the piece will be read increases exponentially—reading can then occur over days or maybe even months.

Accordingly, as you go longer, you'll also need to include subtle reminders to help the reader in case they have forgotten what you wrote earlier or they have skipped ahead.

Rule of Three

In longer-form writing, the rule of three is a good way to think about your writing. It may or may not be appropriate when you come to write, but it can help. The rule-of-three structure works as follows:

Part One: Preview

Start with a preview. Tell the reader what you are going to tell them. Set the context.

Part Two: Content

Having set the context, provide the information.

Part Three: Review

Having provided the information, review and summarize what you have just imparted.

The rule of three is a simple structure that should not be taken as dogma. It helps, but it may not be useful for short posts. Equally, the structure should not override the basic principles of attracting and holding attention.

Sections/Chapters

Sections and chapters are a hierarchical level up from headings.

Sections and chapters as a notion are pretty much interchangeable. You can argue subtle differences, but the practical aspects are virtually indistinguishable. Accordingly, I use both terms, but for this section, I will use the term *chapters*.

The purpose of a chapter is to collate several chunks of information that—when taken together—form part of a larger cohesive whole. Each chapter should be largely capable of being freestanding. In other words, it should be possible to read a chapter on its own without any context outside of that chapter. It should require no previous knowledge and should require no additional knowledge to bolster the central idea of the chapter.

When we learn, we consume information in small chunks, each chunk seemingly independent of others. We learn the chunks and we accumulate. To take that chunked learning to a higher level, we need to synthesize the constituent parts to form a larger whole, that larger whole having new interlinks and relationships between each separate chunk.

To influence, you need to be able to break your argument down into bite-sized chunks, but you also need to provide a structure such that the reader can synthesize the chunks and understand the larger argument.

Headings and subheadings allow you to break down the information into chunks and then chapters allow you to bring those chunks together to provide the synthesized whole. Both techniques are vital for reader understanding.

With each chapter, think about the rule of three. Begin the chapter with a preview, include the main content of the chapter as you expect, and then end the chapter with a review of the material covered. This review may afford you an opportunity to help the reader synthesize the chunks together into a singular, larger block of information.

And lest there be any doubt, the principles for chapters are no different for any other writing—you need to attract and retain interest.

I've Got Some Dull Stuff...

There will be dull stuff.

In case you're wondering, dull stuff is material that the reader won't care about. You might think it's interesting, but if the reader disagrees, then you are wrong. The reader may disagree for the wrong reasons—but they're still right and you're wrong.

It's not a question of whether there is dull stuff; there *always* will be dull stuff—this will particularly be so when business reports are involved. Business reports are generally an excuse to write poorly, to add in lots detail (just in case), to use a lot of jargon (because someone thinks it sounds good and no one else wants to remove it for fear of giving offense or showing their ignorance), and generally to confuse the heck out of the reader because no one has edited the document since some arbitrary deadline has been passed.

When contemplating where to position the details, you need to determine whether:

- The dull stuff is material that actually matters—for example, supporting data.

- The dull stuff is there only because you want to say it, and not because the reader wants to read it.

In the latter case—material that is only there because you want to say it—be brave. Delete the rubbish and move on.

In the former case—where you need to provide this material, even if the reader may not yet realize why—then you need to provide it, but move it out of the way. Put it in an appendix or a separate document. Put it somewhere that the reader can ignore it, but can search it out if needed.

If there is anything that the reader needs to read—in other words, if within this morass of dull stuff, there are a few nuggets that would aid the reader's understanding—then take the nuggets and place them where they are needed. Anything else, get it out of the reader's line of sight.

Building on the Structure

In the previous chapter we looked at identifying the reader—the person whom you are trying to influence. Once you understand whom you are communicating with, you can structure your message for that person.

Structure is both a matter of process—attract attention, hold attention, communicate, influence—and a matter of guiding the reader so that the conclusion—in other words, your influence—is inevitable.

Once you've got your structure in place, it's time to move on and start writing.

Chapter 3

What: Starting to Write

The process of writing is both additive and subtractive. We start with a blank page (or blank screen) and add words. Then we subtract words as we edit.

The process from blank page to publication is a constant push/pull of adding, subtracting, and moving in an attempt to get the right words in the right order. Any word not in the right order is a wrong word and should be cut. The word or phrase or idea might be good, but if—because of the context—it's wrong, then it needs to go.

But before we can edit, we need to get some words down.

Getting to the Words

Writing with the intention of influencing is not a matter of simply writing text. It's not a matter of getting words on the page and ensuring that certain key aspects have been addressed.

To influence with words, you need to present information in a deliberate manner with definite intended results. We're not here to entertain or to show off our writing skills, nor to prove how witty we are. We're writing long-form text with the purpose of making our point understood immediately and in a manner that triggers action.

The words you choose are secondary. If you're expecting an outcome, then it's important that you have something to say.

So ask yourself, do you have something to say?

Or are you simply feeling in need of a rant? Maybe you're repeating something someone else said that you feel needs to be rewritten (or written again) by you?

Do you have something to say, and can you back that something with cold, hard facts? Do you have real firsthand evidence, or are you going to rely on bland platitudes ("it is well known that...")?

If you've got something to say, start writing. And start with the basic unit of communication.

The Basic Unit of Communication

The difference between bad writing and good writing is as simple as understanding the paragraph.

There are no rules in this book, but the use of the paragraph is about as close as you're going to get to a rule. Until you understand what a paragraph is and how to use it, you will not be able to write. You might be able to type, but not write, and you certainly won't be able to wield any influence.

Paragraphs, the Governing Principles

The basic unit of communication is the paragraph. Every paragraph must adhere to a few basic principles:

- A paragraph contains a single thought.

- If there's more than one thought, split the paragraph into its component parts—one thought per paragraph.

- Paragraphs are short (they contain only a single thought). A paragraph can be a single sentence. A paragraph can contain multiple sentences. However, the maximum word count for a paragraph is one hundred words.

Why these governing principles? Because we're creating chunks of information that are easy for the reader to consume. Anything bigger than one hundred words is, metaphorically, too large to fit in a reader's mouth.

We then put the chunks in the correct order, within a structure of headings and subheadings, and group the heading themes into sections and chapters in order to make our wider point. The building block—the quintessential core—is the paragraph.

As an aside, as the writer, if you focus on short pieces of information, it greatly increases the quality of your writing. By focusing on a short chunk with a constrained word count, you really do make sure your idea is clear.

There's another aspect here. Bluntly, if you can't make your paragraphs adhere to these principles, you don't have a grasp on your subject and the essence of what you are trying to communicate, and you don't have a full understanding of the influence you are trying to wield. If you don't have a grasp on your subject, stop writing. Stop writing and go back and learn what you need to learn. Once you have learned you subject, *then* consider influencing.

It's a Binary World Out There

I jest with the heading, of course. One reason to set down our thoughts in writing is because issues are not binary—it's not simply a case of yes/no, either/or, left/right, good/bad. We're dealing with shades of gray and nuance.

However, when we start breaking our longer thoughts into chunks, then each chunk considers a smaller scope of detail, and with that narrowed scope we have the opportunity to provide a more straightforward view. When you get to provide information at the paragraph level, you should be aiming to be definitive in what you say. There should be no ambiguity, and nothing should be predicated on anything else.

I'm not suggesting that nuance and detail go away, simply that when writing paragraphs, the writer should be taking advantage of every opportunity to give the reader unambiguous information. Straightforward information is far easier to comprehend, and the reader will be far more likely to be influenced by arguments laid out in a clear manner.

Of course there will be times when you need to reflect—on one side *this*, but on the other side *that*—but when you can be definitive, be definitive.

Sentences

You might be thinking that the sentence is the basic unit of communication. If you do think this way, you're wrong.

A sentence is a base element, where a paragraph is a fleshed-out thought. A sentence is not viable on its own, or at least it is not required to be viable. Clearly, where a sentence is an entire paragraph, a sentence is a fleshed-out, bite-sized chunk of information, but it is not required to be—it is simply a component part.

Sentences should be short. How short? Read the sentence out loud—if you can't complete it in one breath and without straining/rushing, then it's probably too long. That said, provided you have the skill in word-wrangling, don't be afraid to go long.

However, whether you go long, go short, or do something in between, think about your reader. The sole function of a sentence is to communicate information to your reader as a component part of a chunk of information (a paragraph). You're not trying to demonstrate your writing skill, but to convey information. Three short sentences will likely convey information in a far more digestible manner for the reader than one long sentence with several interlinking subclauses.

Really take some time with your sentences and think about the reader. The reader doesn't want to work at reading—the reader wants to work at consuming new information that will make their life better. If a reader is tired or has to struggle to parse each subclause and figure out which subject applies to which object, then they'll pass and read something else.

If the reader passes, then influence is gone.

Affirmative

When you start crafting sentences that will fit together into paragraphs, write each sentence in the positive. Avoid the negative (and yes, I do get the irony).

Negative isn't simply saying *not* and *do not*. Negative includes an implied negative construction, so for instance, *avoid* is as negative as saying *do not*, even though it would appear that *avoid* is far more affirmative. The practical effect is still the same.

The prime reason to avoid any negative construction is ambiguity.

The opposite of a negative is not a positive. The opposite of negative is just different. The aim in writing (bluntly) should be to tell the reader what they should do. Telling the reader what *not* to do does not tell them how they should behave. A negative construction does not set any expectations or give any guidance.

For example, if you want to tell a reader to walk on the path, say: "Walk on the path." If you say: "Do not walk on the grass," then you leave the matter open to interpretation. The reader could run or jump on the grass—neither is walking. Equally, the reader may climb a tree, which may be another outcome you were not expecting.

Clearly, "walk on the path" is open to some interpretation, but this phrase is far clearer in setting expectations. It is clear that the reader is intended, first, to walk (not run, jump, hop, or whatever), and second, to remain on a delineated area (the path). While there may not be absolute precision (for instance, is someone in a wheelchair only allowed to walk?), the message communicated is far more succinct and is much more accurate in the expectations.

I said the prime reason to avoid any negative construction is ambiguity. The secondary reason is that people tend not to hear the negative—they focus on the positive element of the sentence. So, for instance, if you write "I do not believe in torture," the reader will instinctively read "I believe" (in other words "I *do* believe in torture"). The reader will also be pondering why you're bringing up the subject (in the case of torture) if it's not something for which you at least have some sympathy.

There will be times when only a negative instruction is appropriate ("Do not touch the live rail"), but most of the time, rephrase the negative to the positive. As always, think how the reader will interpret the words. It is much harder to misunderstand an affirmative command than it is a negative construction.

Avoid Punctuation

It's maybe rather extreme (not to mention a negative construction) to suggest avoiding punctuation, but if you can, don't rely on anything beyond a full stop.

Readers understand the full stop. Some readers have difficulty with other punctuation marks, and if you include punctuation, some readers will struggle and may find nuance you did not intend.

While punctuation can aid comprehension, if your sentence needs help, then the best solution is to make the sentence shorter.

If the meaning of your sentence can change based on the presence or the precise placement of punctuation, then rewrite the sentence. Making the meaning dependent on punctuation means that you are dependent on the reader—and every reader—understanding the nuances of punctuation for their interpretation. Not to mention, this assumption presumes your grasp of the rules of punctuation is correct and there are no typographical errors. Even if you get the punctuation correct, if a reader misinterprets the punctuation, then your communication will be lost and your influence will be ineffective.

It's fine to include commas, but review the sentence as if the commas were not present. If the text alone does not fully express what you are intending to express, then rewrite. If there is any doubt, rewrite the sentence.

And just to really hammer this point home: I know how to use a comma, a colon, a semicolon, and an em dash. I'm sure you do too. If there's anyone who's unsure about their use, the style guides offer help. My point, however, is that many readers do not understand the nuances of punctuation, so remove anything that might lead to ambiguous interpretation.

Bold and Italic

If you look at the style guides, they'll tell you the appropriate uses for bold and italic. However, your reader likely won't understand those nuances. Without checking, could you set out the universally agreed rules of when to use bold and when to use italic? I'm not sure I could.

Use bold, use italic if you must, but if you're relying on bold or italic text to differentiate between the same text non-bold or non-italic, then you've got a problem. Use bold or italic as a hint to the reader that you are emphasizing a point, but ensure that the point is fully made in the text.

In short, bolding and italicizing don't make any material change, so don't write as if they do.

Lists

Used in the right place, lists are a great tool, and readers really like lists.

The time to deploy lists is when you have a (short) finite number of points, and those points should be taken as a whole. So, for instance, you may have your three top tips for sharpening a pencil.

Each list item should be short and self-contained. The item can be a single sentence or up to a paragraph. If a list item spans more than a paragraph, you're not really listing.

The list can be numbered, lettered, or bulleted. The form doesn't matter, although there can clearly be an advantage to numbering when there are sequential steps, when the number of items on the list is significant, or if you want to later refer to one (or more) of the list items.

However, lists should be used judiciously and only when necessary. At all other times, use regular paragraphs.

Building Your Paragraphs into Something Bigger

In the previous chapter, we looked at structure. Now we need to start building—we move from the overview to build. In other words, we're going to start filling in the gaps in the frame that we've created.

The process of building is moderately straightforward: write one paragraph, then another, then another, and make sure each one follows the previous while linking to the next.

And just in case you're wondering, there are no rules about the order you write in. You can write the end section first, the middle section three weeks after you write the opening line, and so on. What matters is that, first, you get your key points down (in a form that the reader will understand), and second, you edit the document such that it provides a single, coherent narrative that reads well.

Pacing and Basic Structure

The aim in writing should be to move the reader swiftly through the subject, but not too swiftly. Move the reader swiftly by removing any extraneous fluff and getting straight to the point. However, in getting to the point, don't skip any details or context that is necessary for the reader to understand the point you are making.

And remember, move the reader swiftly and remove anything that's unnecessary first because you respect your reader's time, and second to make sure the point that is being made is crystal clear (and not obscured by superfluous nonsense).

Outline/Summary

I've already mentioned the rule of three, and when you begin writing, begin with the first leg: summarizing what you are about to tell the reader. Don't hint or tease—tell the reader what you have to say at the very earliest opportunity. If you're breaking your work into sections, explain what you have to say at the beginning of each section and give a broad overview at the very start of the document.

Avoid background. Avoid explanation about how you came to be writing what you're writing. Start with what you have to say and include only enough context as is necessary for the reader to understand what you're saying.

Once you've told the reader what you're going to tell them, then you can move on to the detail.

Laying the Foundation

If you've ever watched the construction of a building, you'll know that (conventionally) each level is finished before the next begins. First, the foundations are dug, then the hard core and cement base are added, and the bricks begin to be laid. Each course of bricks is added before the next layer so that the building grows at a uniform rate.

With writing, the approach is different. Dig only enough foundation as is necessary for what you're trying to explain. When you have more to build, then dig more foundations.

Building

Having dug only the necessary foundation and laid only the necessary hard core, then build, and build tall and thin.

Once you've built one tall thin strip, build the adjoining strip. Instead of building horizontal courses, create vertical strips. And keep on with this process until the basic structure is complete.

Detailing

Once you have the structure, then look to the detailing. In practice, this means get the main content communicated.

If you're breaking your work into sections, get most of the section explained. Detailing is what comes on top, only after the basics are secure.

So where does the line get drawn between structure and detail? Clearly, there's a continuum, but detail is any material that, if cut, wouldn't change the essential nature of the section.

Review

And finally, following the rule of three, summarize and review.

Remind the reader what you've just told them, but also link more widely, making explicit the connections to other sections.

Tell Me What It Means

It's very easy to recount facts. Facts are knowable, provable quantities.

She is six feet tall is a provable fact—all that is necessary is a tape measure (and, of course, the person to measure).

However, simply listing facts does not help your reader. We know she's six feet tall...but so what? Is that a good thing or a bad thing? Would something be different if she were taller or shorter?

A fact given without context is irrelevant. If you give a fact, explain the significance and context to the reader. The most straightforward way to think about explaining the fact is to use the construction "which means that...."

So, *she is six feet tall, which means that she can reach the top shelf. She is six feet tall, which means she does not have to stoop when she walks through a doorway.*

You don't need to use those precise words (which means that...), but the explanation is necessary. The link from knowable fact to implication *for the reader* should always be explicit.

Context and Specificity

In order to influence, you need to communicate specific points to your reader, but in order to be specific, those points need to be set in the correct context. Equally, specifics become unimportant based on context.

Let me give you an example: say an inch (25mm) of rain fell in a period of ten minutes. That's quite specific. But if everyone is inside and dry, the context negates the significance of specifics.

However, if you're talking about rain to try to make a point about drainage, then you haven't been sufficiently specific—you need to equate rainfall over time to the quantity of water that would then flow into the sewage system. That inflow can then be compared against the capacity of the drainage system. In other words, in this secondary context, the necessary specifics have not been included.

Let me give you another example: how far is it to New York? That's a simple question, right? So what's the answer?

Maybe it's not so simple—first you need some context:

- Starting from where? A distance is from the starting point to the destination. The destination is New York, but you don't know where the reader thinks the starting point is (because you haven't given the reader that information).

- When you say New York, do you mean New York City or New York state?

- If you mean city, then which borough?

- If you mean Manhattan (to pick one borough), where within that borough do you mean? Central Park, Times Square, somewhere else?

You can keep breaking the geography down until you reach a specific location, but there are other issues to contemplate:

- Which route?

- What other factors will influence the answer? For instance, the method of transport. Equally, there may be major obstacles depending on the route or specific method of transport.

Depending on the context, the reader may not want to know *how far*, but rather *how long until* they reach the destination. Linguistically, one question may have been asked, but the expected answer may be different. Understanding the expected answer requires knowledge of the reader and that the information be relevant and contextualized.

Any data given as raw data (for instance, 23 miles) is irrelevant without an understanding of the context for which that data is the right answer, so either contextualize the specific or delete the information.

Equally, don't assume knowledge. While your primary reader may be knowledgeable and will understand the context:

- Your primary reader may not understand that you have that knowledge and—if you don't include context—may question whether you have correctly contextualized your findings.

- Secondary readers may lack your primary reader's understanding.

Write Less; Write Fewer Words

As you move from paragraphs to chapters/sections and the entire piece, focus on minimizing the length of your message. The shorter your message, the more likely it is to be read.

If your message is ten words long, then there's a very good chance that it will be read. However, if your message is a hundred thousand words long, then—even with the best will in the world—it is unlikely to be read by more than a few people. There is a continuum, although not perfectly linear, and as you move between those two extremes, you move from being more read to being less read.

If you want to be read, then make your writing shorter. Make it shorter by cutting. Don't simply cut what you think is the irrelevant rubbish, cut the material that has no benefit to the reader. If you can make your case in a hundred words, then make your case in a hundred words. You don't persuade someone more by using more words—you just run the risk of boring them before you get to the point.

Length in writing tends to arise for three reasons—none of which is useful if you want to influence.

The first reason for writing long is advertising. Hard-copy newspapers and magazines need content around which they can sell advertising. Electronic publications put advertising around their articles and intercut articles with ads. The longer the article, the more opportunities there are for advertising, and the more advertising there is, the more income can theoretically be generated.

The second reason for writing long is a lack of real understanding. If the writer does not have a tight grip on their subject, they won't know what they can cut. They'll be imprecise and they'll waffle without understanding that they're waffling.

The third reason for writing long is pomposity—a sense of self-indulgence and a love of (metaphorically) hearing one's own voice. I need add no more.

You will note that none of these reasons improves your chance of influencing your reader. Indeed, they will likely have the opposite effect.

Just because you can go long, that doesn't mean you should. In fact, you should aim to do the opposite and use the fewest words possible, thereby showing courtesy to your reader, showing your grasp of the subject, and making sure you focus on the point of influence.

As for the ideal length of a piece? Anything you write needs to be as long as it needs to be. No longer and no shorter. This concept might be difficult for print publishers (who tend to focus on fixed-length documents), but it's quite a simple concept for real people.

Illustration

Illustrations help a reader "see" what you are talking about. They allow the reader to turn abstract concepts into concrete notions.

Illustrations can take two forms: a textual example or a graphic image.

Textual Examples

You can illustrate in words with an example. So, for instance, you may talk in vague terms about a container to hold water. You could then illustrate this with an example: a bucket. There's no need for a photo; your reader will know what a bucket looks like.

Images

Most obviously, an illustration can literally be an illustration, an image of some sort. This may be a photo, a line drawing, or similar.

An illustration should, by definition, illustrate. It should show the point you're trying to get across. It should not be employed to break up text or to take up space, and neither should a graphic be deployed solely because someone has paid for it (or taken the time to create it).

It's very easy to deploy an image that means something to the writer; however, before you use an image, be certain that it will be understood immediately by your reader. Apply the same level of rigor to making your images understandable for readers as you would to making your text understandable.

Also, before you deploy an image, be certain that you have chosen this route because it is the best way to support your point, and that you have not gone for an image simply because your text sucks.

Show, Don't Tell

There's a mantra in fiction: show don't tell. The principle is good, but this is often an excuse for dreary and excessively descriptive prose.

When you write for influence, the principle of *show don't tell* serves us well.

The reason to show rather than tell is that it gives the reader a firm grip on what you're trying to communicate. It illustrates the point for the reader and allows you to be far more specific about the point you are making.

Ultimately, you will always *tell* in that you will recount a list of facts. The skill to showing is recounting the facts that illustrate the point.

Let's have an example: the car was very fast.

Here I have given the reader a simple snippet of information. The reader has no difficulty understanding what I am saying or the underlying point I am trying to convey. If a five-year-old read the sentence, they would fully and immediately understand the point—the sentence is that clear.

But I've told the reader. I haven't shown.

To show, I need to give the reader information that illustrates my point. For instance: the car could reach two hundred miles per hour.

This line does not tell the reader that the car goes fast—it provides a measure of speed and allows the reader to draw their own conclusion. Not only does it illustrate a measure of speed, it provides evidence and quantifies the information that I want to draw to the reader's attention (that the car was very fast).

It also provides a measure for comparison. So, if fast car A can reach one hundred eighty miles per hour and fast car B can reach one hundred ninety miles per hour, then the reader has an understanding that—on this specific and crude measure—the car I am talking about (which can reach two hundred miles per hour) is better.

Now, of course, giving crude measures does not tell the full story. For instance, of the three cars, one may be very unreliable and unable to move more than half a mile without breaking down, and another may have terrible steering, meaning it can't go around corners. These real-world concerns may mean that the crude measure of speed is irrelevant. However, simply saying that the car was "very fast" does not give any indication of these other practical issues.

To help your reader understand, you need to find the illustrations that support your point.

Hundred-Word Paragraph Limit Implemented

In the previous two chapters, we looked at readership and structure. We've now added content and in particular, the basic unit of communication—the paragraph, a single thought not exceeding one hundred words.

By stringing together a series of paragraphs, each focused on the reader and within a coherent structure, you can begin to influence.

In the next chapter, we'll look at the language you can employ to effect that influence.

Chapter 4

Vocabulary: The Words You Write

You might be surprised that you've reached this far in the book before I've raised the subject of the words we choose. Many would have expected word choice to be on page one of a book about using words to influence.

In the nonwritten world, we understand and are well acquainted with the notion of nonverbal communication. Indeed, much of our day-to-day communication is nonverbal. The same principle applies with written communication.

It may sound crazy to suggest that the words you write don't matter. And it is crazy—the words *do* matter—but not as much as you might think. How you are understood is less about *what* you say and much more about *how* you say it, and the context within which the words are delivered.

For this reason, I have spent time looking at the reader and building the framework in which those words are delivered. Once you have the framework, then you can choose the right words.

Word Choice

When you come to write, choose the simplest, most straightforward word you can.

Small Words

If you can find a simpler word than the first word you think of, use the simpler word. If you can find a more complex word that will demonstrate your intellectual prowess, use the simpler word. The point of writing is to communicate, and here you're trying to communicate with the aim of influencing. Showing off your knowledge of big words distracts from the mission of influencing.

Complexity does not come through using complex words with a complex sentence construction. Complexity comes through talking about difficult topics with many issues and many angles.

Simple words do not equate to simple concepts. Indeed, when you strip out any confusion created by complex linguistics, simple words allow the complexity of the concept to be seen all that much more clearly. As an aside, if you can only use complexity, then there is probably a problem with the underlying concept you're trying to explain, and if there isn't a problem with the concept, then there's definitely a problem with your understanding.

The main reason, of course, for employing a simple word choice is the reader. Every complex word you employ requires the reader to fully understand the nuance of that word for your influence to have any effect. For instance, are you sure your reader knows what you mean when you say erstwhile? Are you sure erstwhile is a better word choice than former?

You may have the most perfect grasp on language. You may be able to use words in the exact manner that professors of linguistics believe is correct. But there's little point in using this knowledge if the person you are communicating with does not share that deep and nuanced understanding.

If you need big words to make yourself—or your subject—interesting, then stop writing and reassess your life. If you need big words, then your life and your subject are trivial. Stop writing, because no one will care what you've got to say (apart from your mother, and even then I'm not sure—she's probably only indulging you out of kindness and because she really doesn't want to let on that she stopped listening to you years ago).

Ambiguity

Be aware of words that have several meanings. This might be easier to explain with an example—take the word ignorant. Ignorant has two meanings:

- Lacking knowledge

- Rude

Most people use the word ignorant in its first interpretation—lacking knowledge. And there is some nuance here around the interpretation of the word—it can imply a lack of education or a lack of sophistication.

The second meaning—rude—is perfectly correct but is far less commonly used. I would not choose the word ignorant if I wanted to say someone was rude; I would use the word rude. My reasoning here is simple—most people apply the interpretation "lacking knowledge" when they hear the word ignorant. If people want to say that someone is rude, then they will say that the person is rude.

You may be correct in your choice of words according to the dictionary, but if you leave any scope for ambiguity, then your influence will be weakened.

Thesaurus

I recommend you always have a thesaurus at hand.

The point of a thesaurus is to find a simpler, more natural, more widely understood term or a more precise term. It's not there to search for complications and color.

Emoji/Emoticon

Emojis and emoticons have a place in modern communication. They allow us to communicate complex emotions in a simple form. A happy face can communicate happiness, warmth, agreement, sympathy, reassurance, and more, all in one click of a button.

On a one-to-one level, emojis and emoticons can be the perfect tool to communicate, especially:

- When you don't know exactly how to phrase what you're trying to say

- When you don't know exactly what you want to say

- When you need to say something in the fewest possible characters

While these tools are great for one-to-one communication, there are potential downsides to using them for one-to-several communications. These downsides don't rule out their use, but you should be highly judicious with their deployment.

The first challenge is you cannot always control how the emoji/emoticon is rendered—in the same way we have different fonts, there are different emoticons. This can mean, for instance, that a face that looks cute to you appears sinister to the reader.

Equally, it can be hard to quote the text including the emoji/emoticon, especially when the reader is trying to cut and paste.

In some situations, the emoji/emoticon can mess with the line height, making the text appear odd.

Each reader will apply their own interpretation to an emoji/emoticon. This is perhaps the biggest challenge, since any emoji/emoticon may be viewed differently by different people, and the nuance you're trying to convey may be misconstrued. Equally, some readers see the inclusion of emojis or emoticons as trivializing the text. I disagree—I think these emojis/emoticons add richness to communication—but that doesn't mean everyone agrees that I'm right.

While I am in favor of emojis/emoticons in specific (and limited) circumstances, I don't think they should be used if they're intended to contradict or put a different spin on your text. So, for instance, if you're writing something that is intended to be sarcastic (and I'll get to the topic of sarcasm in more detail later), then don't rely on an emoji or an emoticon to convey the sarcasm (or any other form where what you say isn't meant to mean what you say). If the reader doesn't understand the emoji/emoticon, they will be left with the view that the text you have written is what you intended to say. If you're trying to be sarcastic, then it is likely that the text will say the exact opposite of the meaning you were intending to give.

Similar-Looking Words

Many words may be viewed as difficult. Any word that the reader does not immediately understand as it is used is a difficult word. One special category of difficult words is words that look and are spelled similarly, but have very different meanings.

Take as an example inter and intra or micro and macro. Are you sure your reader will understand the difference between an intercompany transfer and an intracompany transfer? Are you sure every reader fully grasps the difference between microeconomics and macroeconomics?

In both cases the concepts are different. But does your reader fully grasp the difference without needing to think? Have you removed any scope for misunderstanding or confusion?

If you talk about a transfer between companies (rather than intercompany) and a transfer within a company (rather than intracompany) your message will be clearer. Equally if you talk about consumer economics (assuming that is what you actually mean when you mention microeconomics) and economics of the nation (assuming that is what you mean when you mention macroeconomics), then you will find less scope for confusion (and less scope for typing/autocorrect errors).

Nouns and Verbs, Not Adverbs and Adjectives

I agree. I disagree. I vehemently disagree.

What's the difference between *disagree* and *vehemently disagree*?

Nothing. Both are not agreeing.

Adding the adverb, vehemently, is bringing emotion and often with that emotion comes a value judgement, essentially implying the writer really, really, really disagrees because there is something morally wrong.

In this example, the addition of the adverb gives no further useful information. As with the addition of most adverbs and adjectives, all it shows is the writer's values. The values the writer holds dear do nothing to help influence the reader, even if they are matters that the writer believes to be fundamentally important.

Adverbs and adjectives have a place in our language, but that place is generally not when you're seeking to influence. If you feel your noun or verb is weak, the better course is to choose a stronger noun or verb, not to bolster a weak word with another weak word.

Implied Value Judgements

Adverbs and adjectives can bring implied value judgements, but so too can the choice of nouns and verbs.

Let me give you an example. Say you are writing a report and you want to raise a problem with the accounts for the fourth quarter. Did you see the value judgment I slipped in there? I mentioned a *problem*. I didn't say what the problem is—I simply stated that there is, without question and without doubt, a problem.

The assertion that there is a problem brings up several questions. What makes this a problem? Who is this a problem for? And of course, we can go further and wonder: is it a problem or, more accurately, an annoyance, a catastrophe, or a disaster?

Clearly there is something here, but by choosing to apply a value-based label, whatever is being communicated is not necessarily being communicated correctly. The writer may believe that *problem* is the correct label, but the reader may disagree.

A less judgmental description may be to use a term such as aspect, consideration, or issue (although the word issue can be used euphemistically to imply a problem). So, for instance, you could talk about the issue with the accounts or an aspect that needs a more detailed review. The function—drawing the reader's attention—is maintained, but you are treating the reader like a responsible person who is capable of investigating and making up their own mind.

Bringing value judgements may stop a reader from reading. The moment the writer's view diverges from the reader's view is the moment the reader will feel the incongruity. And once the reader notices the incongruity, they won't be paying attention to the content.

This arises when the writer is saying what the writer wants to say, rather than expressing what the reader needs to hear. It is also the point at which the writer has stopped thinking. The writer believes they are correct—there wouldn't be a value judgment unless the writer believed their judgement was correct. This is an arrogant and ignorant position for the writer to adopt and could stop any further communication.

There is no good. There is no bad. There simply *is*. Recount the facts without color and let the reader form their own opinion. Influence comes through the arguments you are laying out, not through distorting the facts.

Pronoun

We use pronouns frequently. These are words—he, she, him, her, they—used instead of nouns (or phrases). So, instead of saying "Steve's car," we might say "his car." We use pronouns because the repetition of the noun (Steve) gets tedious quickly.

Nonspecified Pronouns

Pronouns are deployed liberally in writing, and this is often a good thing. However, it can readily lead to confusion. The most frequent confusion is in understanding which noun has been replaced by the pronoun.

For a pronoun to work, the noun that is being replaced must be understood. This requires context. If I had simply said "his car," you wouldn't be able to ascertain that I meant Steve's car, unless I had already mentioned Steve and it was obvious that the ownership of the vehicle related to that specific individual (and only that individual).

But often when talking about more nebulous concepts—thoughts, ideas, beliefs, theories, and so on—pronouns become troubling. Assertions are made that are very clear and very assertive—for instance, "this is designed to be fast"—but the noun related to the pronoun is sometimes not even clear to the writer. A pronoun in this instance is often used as a grouping term.

Pronoun Confusion

When writing, we're used to pronoun confusion, which can happen when there are too many similar pronouns. For instance, if you're writing about three men, it can be hard to be specific about which man you mean when you say "he." The usual response to this confusion is to liberally insert the noun, so instead of "he," you say "John" or "James."

This can work and remove confusion on the part of the reader. As an aside, notice what I did there with the slightly fuzzy pronoun "this."

However, pronoun confusion is usually an indication of a more significant challenge in the content you're trying to convey. Rather than simply exchanging nouns for pronouns, consider rewriting in a simpler fashion. So, if you are writing about three women, write three sentences—one sentence covering each woman.

Using a Good Word Badly

There's a real allure to using good words, but often these words can be used badly. The writer likes the sound of the word, but then deploys it in a manner that leaves the reader understanding each individual word in a sentence but unable to fathom what the sentence is actually intended to mean.

Using precise words doesn't guarantee you'll be understood—readers will still interpret text how they want—but at least you'll stand a chance of being understood.

However, using the wrong words—using words that mean something different from what you are intending to say—guarantees that you won't be understood by readers in the manner you intend. If the reader is somehow meant to understand through telepathy what you were thinking when you wrote something—and to understand something that is different from what is written—then you're unlikely to see your words have the influence you may have intended.

Let's look at some examples of this.

Jargon and Idiom

Jargon is specialized words or expressions, often used by a profession or closed group, which are difficult for others to understand. An idiom is an expression whose meaning cannot be inferred from the meanings of the words constituting that expression.

Jargon and idioms are also pretty impenetrable to the group members using the jargon and idioms.

Jargon has a place. It is helpful in adding precision. Jargon may be able to express precisely and succinctly a concept or notion that would require an entire paragraph to explain.

If you can be certain you're using jargon with its correct meaning and you've placed the terms within the necessary context, and if you can be certain that every primary reader and secondary reader understands the jargon terms and that no other reader will see the text, then please go ahead and use jargon.

Idioms should be avoided, especially when you are involving nonnative speakers of the language who will likely lack the cultural context.

When Not to Use Jargon

Jargon tends to have a fuzzy, somewhat imprecise meaning. Or rather, jargon tends to be slightly misunderstood by many people.

Because jargon is usually applied to something where specialized knowledge is a prerequisite, that knowledge prerequisite excludes people from understanding. People with a patchy knowledge have a tendency to use jargon—often in an attempt to show their knowledge—but will not fully understand the implications of the term that is being used. If that fuzzy understanding is then communicated to a reader who also has a fuzzy understanding, then there is no way the reader's understanding will be improved.

Clearly, the simplest approach here is to remove all jargon and to state in simple terms what you intend to state. And generally, if there is a broad audience, this is the best course.

However, if there is a narrow audience—for instance, if your audience is mainly made up of experts who would understand the term—you may want to use jargon, if for no other reason than many readers will be left wondering why you didn't mention that specific aspect or use a word/phrase they were expecting.

The better course in this event is to use the jargon in conjunction with an explanation. For example: jargon—in other words, the use of specialized terms that may be meaningless to outsiders—can be used.... Alternately: The use of specialized terms that are understood by few (jargon) should be avoided....

By including a brief explanation, the writer can clearly telegraph to the reader what they mean. For the expert reader, the writer can telegraph that they fully understand the jargon and all the implications bound up with that term. For the lay reader, the writer can explain the basic concept they are referencing. This approach achieves the clearest and broadest understanding in your readership, and once your readers understand, then you can move to influence.

But on the whole, less jargon is better. And if you think you're not using jargon, just ask yourself whether your grandparents would understand what you have written. If there would not be an immediate understanding of every term you have used, then your words need to be edited.

New Words and Imprecise Words

Language is fluid. The meaning of words change over time, and new words are added to our vocabulary. But new words often take a while until their meaning is widely understood. Let me give you an example.

Take Google, the US technology company owned by Alphabet. Google is perhaps best known for its search engine, also called Google. But from Google the search engine, we now have the verb: to google. On the face of it, we understand the verb to google. But when we look harder, what does *to google* actually mean? For instance, does the verb *to google* mean:

- To use the Google search engine?

- To follow the business practices of the company Google?

- To search for something on the internet?

- To find out for oneself?

- To look for information held electronically?

- To find details using a computer or phone?

With context, we could probably kinda/sorta ascertain what a writer meant by the term "to google," but it's certainly not a term where there is no room for ambiguity.

This is just one example of many new and/or imprecise words. If you mean something, then say what you mean, don't poke at it with stick and hope the reader catches on.

Ization and Ification

Adding -ization and -ification to words is another form of jargon and imprecision.

You've doubtless seen this practice, where nouns are taken—Manhattan or app—and then treated as verbs, but the verbs are then made into these new sort of nouns: Manhattanization or appification.

Generally, this is a horrible practice because:

- It first transforms a noun into a verb. However, that transformation is implied, and the precise meaning of that verb is unstated.

- Then, the verb is converted back to a noun.

Let's take an example. People talk about the Manhattanization of London.

To understand this phrase, you need to understand which Manhattan is being referenced (do we mean one of the many places called Manhattan, the drink, the ship, or another application), and once you are sure you have the correct Manhattan, then you need to clarify the very specific characteristic of Manhattan that is implied.

In this instance, the Manhattan being referenced is Manhattan, New York, an area of thirty-something square miles and with a population of more than 1.5 million. The precise characteristic of Manhattan is less clear.

The characteristic could be the presence of a financial district, the fact that it's part of a bigger city, the location next to a river, the fact that it's a major city but not the capital, the density of population, the air quality, the yellow cabs, and so on. There is nothing inherent in the word Manhattan that implies an interpretation.

However, in this case, the characteristic is having many skyscrapers in a small area. So, to talk about the Manhattanization of London is to refer to the current trend (over the last five or so years, at the time of writing) to build tall buildings in London in a comparatively limited area.

But you'll also see there is much scope for ambiguity—how tall do the buildings have to be? How small must the area be and how densely packed must the towers be? In other words, even if your reader understands the basic concept of Manhattanization, there is still no empirical measure by which to test whether London is being Manhattanized.

There are many new words out there. If you're writing for influence, choose the old ones that everyone understands.

Euphemism

Euphemisms are, in essence, another form of jargon or idiom. A euphemism is a word or phrase that requires a prior knowledge and context to understand.

A euphemism is a substituted word or phrase intended to soften the underlying truth. For instance, "He has a colorful past" might be a euphemism for the truth—that he spent five years in jail, having been convicted of fraud.

As with all instances of not writing exactly what you mean, euphemisms should be avoided. Instead, simply recount the basic facts and let the reader make up their own mind.

This is not to suggest that a writer should never seek to soften a hard message, simply that adding confusion and imprecision is not necessarily the way to achieve that desired softening.

Imprecision

It's very easy to be imprecise. Ironically, it's even easier to be precise.

As a writer, if you're precise, you don't need to consider whether your description is correct or fair. If your description is accurate, it will always convey the correct meaning to the reader.

So, for instance, if you say "There were many people in the room," this will convey something to the reader. The imprecision in this phrase is the word *many*. What does many mean? Is many three? Is many twelve? Is many a function of density, so you need more people in a bigger room, if those people are to be accurately described as *many*?

I don't know the answer to these questions, and neither will your reader. However, if you say "There were seven or eight people in the room," then the reader will immediately understand what you mean.

As with most writing, cluttered and imprecise text is usually the symptom of cluttered and imprecise thinking. If you're unsure what to write, the problem is unlikely to be the text—the issue is more likely to be associated with the matter you intend to communicate.

Abbreviations and Acronyms

Some abbreviations and acronyms have become more widely understood than their expanded variant. For instance, do you know what the letters BBC, NATO, and AIDS stand for? Are you certain your reader would understand?

In any situation where you are confident that the abbreviation or acronym is better understood than the expanded version, then use the abbreviation/acronym. Most people haven't heard of the North Atlantic Treaty Organization, but they know what you mean when you write NATO.

If the reader may not immediately understand the abbreviation or acronym, then use the full form. Equally, if there's any ambiguity—for instance, if it's not clear within the context of what you're writing whether the CIA you're talking about is the Chemical Industries Association or the Central Intelligence Agency—then on first use, use the full form rather than the abbreviation.

There's a subset of abbreviations that are widely used but frequently misunderstood. You will know these: "ie," "eg," and "ex" to give three examples. The difficulty here is that unless you know what these letters mean, you'll struggle to understand. The answer to this challenge is simple—say what you mean.

So, if you mean "for example," say *for example* and not eg. If you mean "that is to say" or "in other words," then say *that is to say* or *in other words*, rather than ie.

And if you mean "for example," never say ex. Ex means former (for example, ex-wife). If you want to use ex to mean for example, the correct form is "ex gr," but no one will ever understand what ex gr actually means, so stick with the words *for example*.

These examples (ie and eg) have their roots in Latin. But there are far more problems with this dead language.

Latin

Latin is just another form of jargon, but worse than that, it's a very sneery jargon. Frequently Latin is deployed with pomposity and with the intention of being understood only by those who understand Latin.

Latin requires learning. It is a dead language, so a nonspeaker cannot expect to pick up the language through watching television, reading newspapers, or conversing at the bar. Using Latin therefore excludes anyone who has not had the privilege of a classical education.

Many phrases in English are Latin terms or have Latin roots (etc, et cetera, &c, pari passu, modus operandi, v [versus], ad hoc, ad lib, NB, per se, and ergo, to name a few). None of these words is necessary or helpful if your goal with your writing is to influence.

Drop the Latin, say it in English. There will never be a time when your words will be more clearly understood in a dead language than in simple English. Ever.

To be clear, the study of Latin is valuable if for no other reason than one learns many of the roots of the English language, and there is never any downside to expanding one's knowledge. However, taking knowledge of a dead language and then scattering it within text that is intended to influence is counterproductive.

Legalese

There is a place for written legal language, and that place is legal documents. Legal documents are largely the opposite of writing intended to influence. Often, they are what is created when attempts at influence have failed.

Arcane construction intended to mimic legal documents does nothing to assist the understanding of the reader. Further, an attempt to bring a legal argument into a document that is intended to influence often just highlights the underlying weakness of the argument.

Shakespeare

Shakespeare was perhaps the greatest playwright in the English language. You should go and see his stuff, but keep his text out of your writing.

How does a Shakespeare quote help? What does it add? How does something written as a piece of entertainment by a guy who died four hundred years ago give an insight that you cannot better and more pertinently explain in your own words?

This applies equally for any other quotation you want to mention—what does it add that you cannot better say in your own words?

Also, if you're quoting someone else, you're telegraphing to the reader to expect derivative reasoning and a lack of original thought.

Subtle Differences

The English language is varied and colorful. There are many ways to describe an everyday object. If you want an example of this, think how many words we can use to describe the lavatory.

Getting Hung Up on Word Choice

The range of color in language gives writers choice. Generally we think of choice as good, but too much choice can slow down the writing process and blunt the influence. It's very easy to find two words where the meaning is nearly interchangeable and to spend a lot of time trying to choose the better of the two, whatever better actually means in this context.

While I have stressed the need to choose the word that expresses mostly closely what you want to say, be wary not to get too hung up in these word choices. If you have two words that mean broadly—but not quite exactly—the same thing, the word choice isn't the issue that will determine the reader's understanding or your influence.

The reader will pick up on many signals in the text and take them as a whole. Focus on the finished totality, not on the individual elements that will be invisible to the reader. But make sure you don't use this flexibility as an excuse for poor writing.

Other Nuances

There are many other subtle nuances. Let's be frank—virtually all of those nuances add nothing to the reader's understanding. For instance, is there is a difference in meaning between a word with a capital letter and a word without? If such a subtle nuance is in there, you've missed the point.

Single words—provided you have chosen a word that broadly describes what you intend, have included that word in a coherent sentence, and have spelled the word at least in the ballpark of an accepted spelling somewhere in the world—do not matter. As I've said before, the basic unit of communication is the paragraph—focus on getting your paragraphs right.

Units

Measures and units can be troubling—especially when communicating with someone who thinks in different units.

Take weight (as in the weight of a human being) as an example. In the US, weight is measured in pounds, so a man may weigh 230 pounds. In the UK, we use stone and pounds, where one stone is fourteen pounds. So, in the UK a 230-pound man would weigh 16 stone and 6 pounds. By contrast, in Europe they use kilos to measure weight, and a 230-pound man would weigh 104 kilograms.

As another example, take gallons. In the US there are gallons, and in the UK there are gallons. Trouble is, they are different measures. One US gallon is equivalent to 0.832674 UK gallons.

Where there is any scope for any doubt, talk in the language your reader understands and be clear about the units you are specifying. So, if you are aiming your text at US readers, express weights in pounds—not stone, not kilos—and measure in US gallons—not UK gallons or liters.

Currency

Wherever possible, when you talk about money and financial issues, convert to local currencies.

But don't simply convert the amount, ensure that the illustration is relevant to the market. So, to give a marginally ridiculous example, if average salaries in Germany are €1 million/year but average salaries in the US are $10,000/year, don't simply convert euros to US dollars (or vice versa).

If you talk about salaries, make the currency local and write with an appreciation of local issues. Taking the example above, someone earning $10,000/year will spend a far greater proportion of their earnings on food than would be the case for someone earning €1 million.

Another area to be cautious is where currency has little meaning. In countries hit by endemic corruption, skyrocketing inflation, or war, money is often not the means of trade, so any sort of conversion to local value is likely to offer little understanding.

One other aspect of currencies to keep in mind is commodities that are conventionally priced in a specific currency. For instance, oil is priced in dollars. In these instances, keep the trading currency. But do convert to the local currency when you talk about petrol/gasoline prices that affect citizens.

Fractions and Percentages

What's the difference between five-eighths and two-thirds? Answer... 4.16 percent.

Throughout this book I've emphasized the need for accuracy. However, there's a point at which you can be too accurate. I've also emphasized the need to talk in terms that people understand—and most people do understand basic fractions and percentages, but not enough and not in the way they think they do.

While people intellectually understand fractions, trying to grasp the nuance is difficult. So, if we take the comparison in the first line of this section—five-eighths and two-thirds—those *feel* very different. They feel very different because both the numerator and the denominator are different.

In truth, the two fractions are not dissimilar. Convert them to percentages, and you get 62.5 percent (five-eighths) and 66.66 percent (two-thirds). In other words, you have a difference of just over 4 percent, which is a lot less than one may feel is the difference.

When it comes to percentages and fractions, wherever you can, generalize. If you need to talk about seven-sixteenths, then say "just under half," unless accuracy is absolutely fundamental to your piece (for instance, you're applying for a grant). If you are *accurate enough*, your reader will understand and won't lose interest in your writing while they find the calculator app on their phone.

Probability and Risk

In part our inability to compare stems from a general human inability to link numbers (particularly complex numbers like fractions and percentages) to reality. Sure, we can understand what a 2 percent pay raise means for us, but beyond that, humans are just bad with numbers. Let me illustrate this point further with some probabilities.

Say I told you there was a 30 percent chance of something bad happening. To most people that feels like a very unlikely event; not impossible, but unlikely. You probably wouldn't be too concerned about a 30 percent risk.

But let's look at that risk in another way. Let's look at the risk in terms of flipping a coin, and for this example we'll say that heads equate to *a bad thing* and tails equate to *a good thing*.

If you flip a coin three times, you wouldn't be shocked if it came up heads once and tails twice. A coin being flipped three times and coming up heads once is equivalent to a 33 percent risk, which is pretty close to a 30 percent risk.

Framing the risk in terms of three flips of a coin—rather than as a percentage or a one-in-three chance—makes the risk far more immediate for the reader and makes the assessment of risk far more practical.

A coin flip *feels* riskier, and more significantly, a reader can understand that while there may be a one-in-three chance, there is also a very real chance that the very first flip could be heads (in other words, a bad thing). Equally, the reader would expect that if you kept flipping a coin heads would come up at some point (which may not be the case if you simply talk about a 30 percent risk).

If you can, exclude any discussion of probability and risk, since you will likely send your reader to sleep. But if you do need to include this sort of detail, then link the numbers to something your reader can readily relate to and illustrate with a concept that shows the real-world likelihood.

The Writer's Voice

Every document has a writer (or several writers), but a key question is who do you want your reader to perceive as being the writer?

Establishing the writer of the document is as much about setting the tone, style, and authority of the document as it is about the presence (or apparent lack of presence) of an individual. The authorial voice is part of how you communicate—it is about the subtlety and psychology of the communication as much as the actual words.

There are no hard-and-fast rules for the authorial voice, but the context and the expectations of your reader are likely to be key influencing factors, as is the extent to which you (as the writer) want to make your presence felt.

Perhaps the most significant decision is whether to write in the first person, second person, or third person.

First Person Singular

With the first person singular, the writer is "me." In other words, the form employed is *I notice, I think, I recommend*, and so on.

The advantage of first person singular is that the writing can be very personal. It is possible to adopt a very conversational tone and write as if you were sitting down with the reader, having a chat over a cup of coffee.

The disadvantage is that you can't always honestly speak in the first person singular. For instance, if you are representing a body and speaking on behalf of that body, then it may not be your opinion that is being expressed. That said, if you are speaking on behalf of a body, then you may not want that "chat over a cup of coffee" feel.

From a purely personal perspective, I have a preference for first person singular. It is one human talking with another, and in my opinion, that's the way the world should be. Added to which, I think one can have better influence speaking for oneself rather than speaking for others.

First Person Plural

With the first person plural, the writer is "us," and you will be using the form *we investigated, we understood*, *we were surprised*, and so on, and now we are writing and speaking as one.

This construction gives a very *corporate* feel and brings a certain distance. This can be beneficial, but it is also tougher to make your influence felt since the argument feels as if it is being made by a separate body that isn't party to the discussion. This approach can work, but it is harder.

If you've been paying attention, then you'll notice I've been using "we" quite often. However, I've used we in a different way. I've used it to mean us two: you, the reader, and me, Simon. Us, together.

I have used we in this manner because I am trying to foster a sense of shared mission with you. I genuinely believe we are in this together—you are my comrade in arms, and we are in the trenches fighting the good fight to express ourselves more effectively.

Sometimes you can use we in this manner. Sometimes it works well. I'll leave you to form your own opinion about how well it has worked in this book.

First Person Corporate

Expressing a view on behalf of a body—a company, a statutory body, or similar—is always tricky.

Corporate bodies are singular entities, but as the writer, you can't, for instance, say "I, XYZ Megacorp, have decided..." It just somehow doesn't feel right, added to which, corporate bodies do not generally have the ability to type. There are, however, three main options you can adopt:

- You can use first person singular, expressing yourself (implicitly or explicitly) to be writing on behalf of the corporate body.

- You could also use the first person but express a personal opinion.

■ Alternatively, you can use first person plural and imply that the corporate entity is a somewhat amorphous blob of humanity.

There are certain circumstances where you may be constrained from using some of these options; for instance, often a professional individual (professional in this context being a lawyer, an accountant, a surveyor, an actuary, a doctor, or other member of a professional body) may be required to express their opinion as an individual. This requirement to express an opinion as an individual may be laid down by legislation or by the regulating professional body, and that expression of a personal opinion may have the consequence of personal liability.

Second Person

With the second person, the writer disappears, and instead the focus is on "you." You should do this, and you should do that. The writer is invisible and yet is somehow giving instructions.

Second person is tough to write and often reads like a set of commands. Both of these are good reasons to avoid the perspective. That said, it can work, and you will note that I have frequently used this approach throughout this book. I like to use second person because, to me, provided it's clear that *I* am talking to *you*, it can feel conversational.

I'll get onto mixing the perspective in a moment, but a quick word about first and second person together. If you use a construction of the form "I think you should do...," then you've adopted the first person. You are clearly addressing the reader, but you're writing in the first person.

Third Person

As with second person, with third person the writer disappears, but instead of the focus being on "you," it is on he/she/it/they/the company/the whatever.

Third person gets to be very business speak-y and loses sight of who is talking to whom.

Mixing It Up

There's no law stopping you from mixing and matching any of these options—and there's especially no law stopping you from mixing up the first person options. However, if your goal is influence, it's better if you avoid mixing.

Once you mix, it gets hard to focus. If "I" say you should do this and "we" recommend that, then the reader loses track of who is speaking—the reader may not be able to put their finger on the problem, but they will notice a dissonance. And once the reader starts to wonder who is actually talking to them, they lose focus on the subject. When they have lost focus on the subject, influence ends.

As far as possible, as far as practical, stay with first person singular, and you'll be fine.

Again, you will have noticed that I have mixed my approach—this was a deliberate choice on my part. My intent has been to make the book conversational—I am talking to you—but I wanted to approach the topics from various angles to give a broader perspective, and so I have used different voices to highlight those different aspects.

I've also tried to soften some of my messages—constant use of the second person can feel very hectoring to a reader, and leave them feeling that an author who they have never met is criticizing them directly. Moving from the second person to the first or third person can make it clear that I'm talking about an approach rather than criticizing.

Choosing the Right Words

Simplify, simplify, simplify. And then simplify some more, but don't simplify more than is necessary.

Then once you've chosen the right words, it's time to present your argument.

Chapter 5

Presenting Your Argument

Much of the work in presenting your argument is removing the unnecessary, the extraneous, and the untruthful. And to be frank, you want to get rid of the arguments you're just having with yourself, the arguments with your parents that you're still replaying in your head, and the argument you had with a boyfriend/girlfriend ten years ago.

Once you:

- Know who you're addressing

- Have a structure to your text, and

- Have chosen the right words

you can begin to make an argument in a sensible, logical, and straightforward manner.

In short, if you present your thinking in a questionable way, then the reader will focus on the manner in which you are arguing. The focus will shift from the content to arguing a point. In other words, you will not be discussing the matter on which you want to exert influence, but rather arguing about anything and everything that is irrelevant in the context of the point you want to make.

Basic Principles of Presenting Your Argument

Writing with the intention of exerting influence is different from arguing or debating in public. The point of writing is not to win an argument or a debate—the purpose is to bring new understanding and change minds.

Unlike a debate or face-to-face argument, the written form is a singular communication. In many cases, it's a single opportunity with no option to respond to comments or to clarify. In some cases there may be the chance to asynchronously engage with the reader, but asynchronous engagement is not necessarily the best form of communication if you're trying to clarify a misunderstanding.

Since we're not debating or arguing when we write, most of the rhetorical devices that might be employed when speaking face to face become at best irrelevant and at worst counterproductive. Instead, when writing, a much more straightforward approach should be adopted:

- Make the argument relevant for your reader.

- Get to the point quickly.

- Make your point as succinctly as you can.

- Lay out the facts of your argument—and only the facts. This is not a place for opinion.

- Let the facts speak for themselves.

If the facts don't speak for themselves, the problem that needs to be fixed is not with your writing or the presentation of your argument. The problem is what you're arguing. In other words, you have a problem with the fundamentals, and you need to reassess exactly who it is you're trying to influence and the topic on which you are trying to influence.

One other aspect of influence to remember is that people's opinions often change slowly. If you think you can change an extreme view with a few hundred well-chosen words, you may be disappointed. You may succeed, but the likelihood is that sort of influence will take a while longer, especially if you're trying to change something that is fundamental to someone's identity.

The Incorrect Application of a Good Principle

The incorrect application of a good principle is perhaps the easiest error to make when writing. It's easy because the writer is right in what they are writing—they are expressing a good principle. However, the writer is often blinded to the connection between the cause and effect.

Let me illustrate. Here I am using a slightly extreme example in order to highlight my point. This makes it easier to see the disconnect in the application, but very often that disconnect will be far subtler and far less obvious to identify.

Say you want to influence on the subject of fire safety in tall buildings. In this context, there would be much to discuss, and one area you would likely want to cover would be the human health aspects—not simply the risk of fire, but how reacting to fire can be a challenge for people with health challenges.

And when you talk about people with health challenges, you might talk about a healthy, balanced diet and the benefit of eating well.

Healthy eating is clearly a good principle—who could argue against healthy eating? But healthy eating is irrelevant in the context of fire safety in tall buildings.

Facts, Opinions, Beliefs, Projections, and Assumptions

We all have opinions. Trouble is, we all tend to think that our opinions are matters of fact, not simply a subjective conclusion.

There is a tendency to work on the basis that our opinions are matters of fact and to then discount any possibility that these opinions may be based on false evidence or false premises. And we certainly never stop to consider the possibility that our opinions may be based on ignorance or incomplete understanding.

Often when we start to write, we are looking for facts to support our opinion when we should first be looking to underlying issues around which we are trying to influence.

While it's nice to suggest that only facts matter, in reality any piece of writing will likely have to include a range of facts, opinions, projections, and other factors where the detail can be questioned.

Facts

If you have a fact to state, then state that fact simply.

That said, one of the biggest challenges with facts is understanding what makes a fact a fact. Any fact can be verified by evidence—one person's (or even several people's) opinion does not constitute evidence.

If you are asserting a fact that is questionable, then it is likely not a fact. What you are putting forward may be reasonable and may be supported by strong logic, but that doesn't make it a fact. Equally, just because you have the element of a fact, that doesn't mean that everything associated with that fact is also true.

Let me give an example of how facts can be blurred with non-facts. Say that someone is found dead... That the person is dead is a verifiable fact.

If the person was shot, that too would be verifiable. If the shot caused the death, that would likely start as supposition—there might be a wound consistent with a shot—but with the benefit of a forensic examination, that supposition can be proved to be fact. However, asserting as fact that the individual was murdered or that a specific person was then responsible for the murder is a much harder task. That is not to say that the question of murder cannot be proved—simply that it is harder to prove, and the fact of the death does not prove there was murder.

If you read Chapter 3, *What: Starting to Write*, you will already be thinking about linking facts to context and implication. So instead of saying "She is six feet tall," you may talk about the implications of the height in the context of what you're discussing: "She is six feet tall, which means she can reach the top shelf...."

If you are making the link from the fact to the implication—and you should; it helps your reader understand and see what you are talking about—then you need to ensure that the implication is factually correct too.

Correct Facts, Wrong Conclusions

I've already talked about the misapplication of a good principle. Taking the correct facts and drawing the wrong conclusions is the parallel. Simply recounting facts correctly does not guarantee understanding or that the facts will be correctly contextualized.

Expressing Opinions

There will be times when you need to express an opinion. But before you express an opinion, consider why you are doing so. Take a moment to ponder how you expressing your opinion will influence another person.

If your opinion is supported by evidence, and you have logically extrapolated that opinion from a fact or several facts, and the opinion will have an effect on the influence, then express your opinion. However, in this event ensure you characterize your opinion as opinion and not as fact.

If, however, you are expressing your opinion because you believe your opinion matters, then maybe consider another approach.

I have previously mentioned the abuse of adverbs and adjectives. Their inclusion is often a way for the writer to express their opinion. Equally, a poor choice of nouns and/or verbs can express an opinion.

Let me give an example. Compare: *"I disagree," he said* with *"I disagree," he shouted angrily.*

Employing a more colorful verb (shouted, rather than said) and adding the adverb (angrily) gives a markedly different perspective on the two words and allows the writer to insert their own opinion and their own contextualization where both are likely inappropriate.

Professional Opinion

Many opinions are based on personal preferences. For instance, if you're in a restaurant and you thought the sauce was too spicy, that is just a personal preference—there is no internationally agreed standard of where "just right" becomes "too spicy," and the cutoff point is (literally) a matter of personal taste.

However, there are times when an individual is required to offer an opinion, and that opinion matters. The most common occurrence is when an individual is required to give their professional opinion. As a reminder, throughout this book I'm referring to a professional as being a lawyer, an accountant, a surveyor, an actuary, a doctor, or another member of a professional body.

The requirement to give an opinion may arise in many situations; for instance, an accountant may be required to express an opinion as to whether a company is solvent, or maybe a lawyer is required to give a legal opinion as to whether a criminal act has been committed.

In these instances, provided it is clear that the opinion is being given in a professional capacity and the terms of the opinion comply with any requirements of the body that governs and regulates the profession, then there should be no hesitation in stating the opinion.

Virtue Signaling

To a greater or lesser extent, we all virtue signal much of the time. Look at any social media post and you will see virtue signaling, not least when people change their profile picture to reflect the latest cause they're showing solidarity with. While the cause may be good, the gesture is frequently empty because the owner of the new profile picture won't be taking any concrete action such as donating their time or money—they're simply displaying their virtue in public.

Virtue signaling happens when we give voice to moral values. It is the conspicuous assertion of moral values, but the assertion is made in order to demonstrate the writer's moral purity to the writer's social group, with the aim of elevating the writer's status within that group.

In other words, virtue signaling is a purely selfish act and has very little to do with the moral issue the writing is pointing at.

When it comes to writing for influence, cut out all virtue signals.

Cut them out because virtue signaling is introducing a moral argument that is not supported by fact. With virtue signals, the writer is being selfish and insecure, making the writing about the writer, and not about the issue around which the writer professes to want to influence.

Projections and Assumptions

The nature of writing for influence is that we want to influence something that will happen in the future—we're not trying to change the past. We are therefore looking forward and—to a certain degree—predicting the future. That prediction might be as simple as suggesting that everything will remain the same unless there is a change, or it might involve a more convoluted prediction.

With any prediction or projection, there is an assumption (or many assumptions).

So, if we go with the suggestion that everything will remain the same unless there is a change, while that may seem like a statement of the obvious, there is in fact an inherent assumption. The assumption is that there are no other factors involved. However, there is always change—some more expected, some less expected. The change can be small (such as the weather) or major (a complete crash of the international financial system).

Some assumptions are implicit, and some assumptions are explicit. If you make assumptions, then state your assumption.

Beliefs

There's a maxim to avoid talking about politics and religion. If you can avoid writing about—or trying to influence around—politics or religion, or any belief-based system, you will make your life easier.

The reason to avoid beliefs is because by their very nature, beliefs are unproven and unprovable. If they were proven or provable, then they wouldn't be beliefs, they would be facts.

To argue with your beliefs or to argue against another's beliefs is unlikely to result in any change. Someone (or you) already has a view formed on the basis of something other than facts and has likely held that belief for a long time. What makes you think you're going to change their mind with a few well-chosen words? You've already got a heap of unreality in the mix—facts won't help you here.

Also, when you write with the intent to influence, avoid assuming your reader shares your beliefs. Rely on facts and you'll make a stronger argument.

A subset of beliefs is fixed opinions. People have made up their mind—often based on emotion and identity—and are not open to reason. You cannot reason away a belief and you cannot reason away a fixed opinion with no factual underpinning. Views may change, but they're never going to change quickly.

Reporting the Unprovable

One other subcategory of fact to be aware of is the unprovable fact. The difficulty with an unprovable fact is that it cannot be distinguished from an opinion.

Let me give an example: "The king was very pleased with the gifts he received from the visiting dignitary."

How can one know—as a provable fact—that anyone, but in this case the king, is pleased? We would expect any king to have good manners and to display the behavior we all associate with pleasure on being given gifts. But unless the king expresses himself to be pleased, how he actually feels is unknowable (and as an aside, even if he does express himself to be pleased, that may be a lie to avoid giving offense).

Rather than divert your reader from the influence you are intending to project, stick with the details that are observable. So, for instance, you might report that the king smiled. You might report that the king paid attention to his gifts and examined them in detail—maybe he had a discussion with one of the dignitaries about one of the gifts in particular.

You could also state that the king *appeared* to be pleased. But beyond that, you're just inviting your reader to question to entire factual basis of what you have written.

Logical Fallacy

When putting forward an argument, we all frequently rely on shaky logical propositions. Indeed, the practice is so common that many logical fallacies are well understood and analyzed in detail, so I won't list them all here.

However, I do want to call out some of the more reprehensible practices. All of these approaches are easy to adopt—we tend to use them unconsciously—and all should be avoided if you are looking to influence with your writing.

If you deploy any logical fallacy—one listed here or one of the many other fallacies—you may feel that you have made your point. You may have a good point that you are intending to make, but the reader will see the failed logic underpinning your argument, and any chance at influence will be lost.

How many of the following logical fallacies have you employed?

No Evidence to the Contrary

Arguing that because there is no evidence to the contrary, the claim must be true (or false).

An example of this might be: "She was last seen walking down the alley on a dark night. Because she has not been seen since, it must be assumed that she was attacked, maybe kidnapped, or possibly murdered."

Reversing the Burden of Proof

Laying the burden of proof on those questioning the original claim.

An example of this might be a claim that I can fly by flapping my ears. When you question this, I then ask you to provide irrefutable evidence that I cannot fly.

For the record, I can't even flap my ears.

Everybody Knows...

Arguing that because many people hold the view, the claim must therefore be true.

Everyone understands this concept, so I don't need an example here, do I?

Correlation and Causation

Arguing that because one provable fact occurred, the subsequent events are caused by that event. To be more accurate, the argument that correlation implies causation occurs when two variables are found to occur together, giving the impression that one leads to the other.

An example of this would be that whenever there is a thunderstorm, I get a headache. This may be true. However, to then take a step forward and suggest that thunderstorms give me headaches may be incorrectly ascribing the cause.

No Logical Connection

In a similar manner to blurring correlation and causation, arguments are frequently built with a lack of logical connection. The conclusion may be true or false, but the logical argument to support the conclusion is false.

This practice is often called a *non sequitur*, although frequently the term non sequitur is applied to any logical fallacy.

Personal Attacks

If you're trying to influence, you want something to change. Often when there is an obstacle to a change, there is someone behind that obstacle—an individual whose decision has resulted in a situation you believe should be changed.

One shortcut to arguing a position is to attack the character of a person holding the opposing view (often called an *ad hominem attack*). This attack may take any number of forms and is not necessarily related to the matter at hand—for instance, there may be an attempt to humiliate the subject with something from their past.

In terms of influence, personal attacks are a weak strategy. Personal attacks are weak strategy because you're attacking a person and their character, and making such an attack tends to reveal more about the writer than about the person being attacked. The attack can also lead to increased sympathy for the person who is attacked, shifting sentiment against your case.

But the bigger reason for avoiding this practice is that personal attacks simply highlight that you have nothing to say. You have no counterargument to make. You are not trying to achieve anything (other than being unpleasant).

Me, Me, Me, Me, Me, Me, Me

One of the biggest challenges of writing for influence is stripping out the writer. Typically, the writer will write about something that matters to them, and as they do each word is infused with the writer's character.

Your Life Story

Your life story might interest you, but unless you're writing an autobiography or memoir, it won't interest the reader.

Your personal anecdotes don't matter. Everybody is influenced by the events of their life (and often the events of the parents and grandparents). Recounting an anecdote doesn't change the situation or make your influence stronger. Occasionally, an anecdote may help to illustrate a specific point, but rarely.

The reader's key concern is what's in it for them. Always ask yourself what benefit accrues to the reader through investing their time and energy to read your words.

You Should Listen to Me Because...

Any call to pay attention because of some special circumstances simply conveys weakness. If you need to—in effect—say that the only reason for someone to pay attention is for a reason unrelated to the core of your message, then you are telegraphing that your argument has no substance.

If you are pleading special circumstances, then either you need to recast your argument or you have failed to hook your reader at the start of the piece. As an aside, if you have failed to hook your reader, your reader won't be reading by the point you start your special pleading. However, if you happen to get lucky and the reader does read your piece, including special pleading may simply lead the reader to question this pleading and thereby shift their focus away from the fundamentals of your argument.

But I'm an Expert

Sigh. One of the biggest challenges to good writing is expertise.

Expert in Subject

An expert—someone who has a qualification or experience in a subject area—may be required to give their expert opinion in writing. In this situation, the need for influence should be minimal—the expert is effectively acting as an adjudicator/oracle, and all that is necessary is to state the case in a clear and succinct manner.

However, there are times when an expert does need to influence, and this is where the writing can become a challenge.

First, there is the presumption of ability. Many experts don't see the disconnect between knowledge of their subject and the skill of communication. Expertise in writing and communication is not acquired by coupling the ability to type with expertise in a specific field.

Second, while experts may have knowledge, they often don't know the extent of the reader's knowledge, nor what the reader wants to know. This can often lead to less clear communication.

Third, if experts feel the need to influence, then this suggests that something is up for challenge. If something is up for challenge, then the matter is beyond their expertise. Now, certainly, the matter that is up for discussion may be based on a projection using the expert's expertise and may be bound up with assumptions that their years of experience have shaped—but a projection is still a projection. Any projection still has a likelihood of being wrong. And if you want to argue that your expertise makes your projection somehow less wrong, you're still putting forward a case that you're wrong.

The Claim of Expertise

We all understand that someone might be an expert in hairdressing, but that doesn't make that person an expert in brain surgery. However, that doesn't stop experts from feeling that their expertise in one area qualifies then to comment in another.

I am an expert and therefore I know what's right for you is just such a wrong-headed notion. It's both arrogant and ignorant, and it betrays a lack of expertise—if someone can profess to know the unknowable, then they're clearly a charlatan.

If the writer's only way to make an argument is to claim expertise—and in so doing to therefore claim that the writer's view has weight beyond the weight of other people's argument—and yet they are not able to clearly articulate why their argument is correct without relying on the notion that they're an expert, then the writer is no expert in their topic or any other.

Strawmen and Hypotheticals

A strawman argument is one that exaggerates, misrepresents, mischaracterizes, or just plain tells lies about the other side's view of a contested matter. If you've ever listened to politicians talking about their opponents' policies, then you will have heard a strawman argument being deployed.

A strawman argument can be powerful. If you can mischaracterize an opposing view in a highly unflattering manner, then it can be hard for people to support that opposing view. However, it's a risky approach because you're building your argument on a lie.

A hypothetical argument is one where a fabricated position is drawn up ("Let's assume everyone has thirteen fingers on their left hand") and then is used as a position for comparison ("Clearly the person with thirteen fingers has the advantage, so we should stop hiring people with four fingers and a thumb").

Both approaches lack any essence of truth and will, at best, lead to people talking past the problem and arguing about something that doesn't actually exist. And from the perspective of written influence, neither approach really works.

Negotiation

To conclude this chapter, a few words on negotiation.

There are similarities and overlaps between negotiation and writing for influence, and there are differences. Sometimes the activities are the same, sometimes they're different. The same but different...it's all about context.

There are basics that are the same—for instance, both processes require extensive information gathering. Both processes require a deep understanding of the other party.

But after that, the approach can be very different. Note that I said *can* be different; it doesn't have to be.

This book is focused on writing (hence the title). It's about laying down concepts in a written form so the writer's thoughts and ideas can be shared and other people can be influenced. Ideas may be laid down in this manner as part of a position paper that may be the start of, or a milestone along the road of, a negotiation.

However, at some point in a negotiation there likely will be face-to-face discussions. While some of the approaches discussed in this book may be appropriate for that context, often they will not be. When negotiations get to the face-to-face stage, while writing may have a place, very often it doesn't when key points are being discussed. After an agreement has been reached, then it will often be documented, but during discussions the lack of a written record can offer useful flexibility.

There are times—and negotiation is one example—when a written approach is the wrong approach. Before you metaphorically put pen to paper, make sure that the written word is the best medium.

Bringing the Pieces Together

Making your argument is theoretically simple, but in practice complex. You need to bring together:

■ All the pieces of your argument

■ At the same time

■ And all pointing in the same direction

to give one central coherent message to your intended reader. It sounds simple, but it takes quite some work.

Chapter 6

Presentation of the Text

The manner in which you present the text you write with the intent of influencing is significant. You may have crafted text that will influence anyone and everyone who reads it, but if you then present that text in a way that makes it literally unreadable, your attempt at influence will fail.

Clearly, very few people present text that is literally unreadable. However, many people don't think hard enough about the link between their text and readability. Too often, they make choices based on aesthetics which ultimately hinder reading.

Assuming you have your paragraph lengths right, when it comes to presentation of text there are three key elements to consider:

- Font choice

- Line height (in other words, line spacing)

- Line length (how much text you get on a line)

I'll look at each, initially focusing on print-related aspects, but before I start, please be aware that there will be times when you can't control the presentation. I'll talk about this lack of control after I've covered the main points.

With each of these aspects, be aware that while you may have good eyesight, you cannot guarantee that is the case for readers. Equally, you may be reading in an optimal environment—again, that environment cannot be guaranteed for readers.

Font Choices

Choosing the right font can be the difference between having a readable and an unreadable font. But there's more to the choice of the font than simply choosing the font face.

There's been a trend in recent years toward clean, crisp fonts, which look very attractive. This can be seen particularly in product packaging. The trouble is many of the principles of product packaging have then been transferred to long-form text production, and the results are mixed (and when I say mixed, I'm being kind and doing that euphemism thing I railed against).

Font Face for Body Text

For your main text—the text that comprises the substance of what you want to say—you have one main decision: serif or sans-serif font. Serif fonts have the decorative adornments at the end of each stroke. By contrast, sans-serif fonts have cleaner, crisper strokes without these additions.

When it comes to font choice, let's make this easy—for body text, go with a serif font face.

This is the simplistic answer, but it's also the better answer. Serif fonts are much easier to read—especially with longer pieces. If you want to hold someone's attention so you can make your case, then choose a serif font. If you choose a sans-serif font, you will lose the reader's concentration sooner.

In practice, if your writing is under one thousand or so words, then you'll be fine with sans serif. But anything much past one thousand words, and you'll do best with a serif font. And if you're wondering which serif font, go with Garamond.

Garamond has its origins in the 1400s, and there's a reason the font has been around for more than five hundred years—it's a really, really good font. It is perhaps the most readable font. If you don't know better, or if you don't want to make a bad decision, just choose Garamond as your font and move on.

There are other choices, but seriously, if you're looking for a clear, readable font, just go with Garamond.

As an aside, if you're reading the print edition of this book, then yup, that's Garamond you're seeing.

If you have any hesitation about what I'm suggesting, try this exercise. Find some text that is at least two thousand or so words long. Print out the text. Print it once using Garamond and once using Futura (and if you don't have these fonts, google "Garamond typeface" and "Futura typeface"—you'll find examples).

Now read each document and decide which is easier on the eye. Note when you start skipping or missing lines. Note when you lose attention. Note which leaves your eyes more tired.

There are other serif choices; for instance, Times or a Times variant wouldn't be the worst choice. Don't let me stop you from investigating—you're not going to get arrested for making a different font choice—but if you want to save time...Garamond.

Font Face for Headings

Your headings do not need a serif font—indeed, as with the print version of this book, a sans-serif font can make a good contrast, and since the headings are short, the reader won't encounter the same eye fatigue they would when using a sans-serif body font.

But if you want to use the same font for the body text and your heading, feel free.

When making your choice of font face and font weight combination in headings, look to ensure that each heading level is clearly delineated. Logically each superior heading level should be more significant than inferior heading levels. The hierarchy of heading levels should be obvious to the reader without the reader needing to apply any thought.

In other words, headings should be bigger (and maybe use more weight) than subheadings. Subheadings should clearly be more significant on the page than sub-subheadings, and so on.

Font Weight

Many fonts come in a range of weights. At the minimum, font sets typically offer two weights—regular and bold. However, newer font sets often add light, ultra-light, semi-bold, and ultra-bold, and perhaps more. These weights give the layout tech a huge range of options.

For the body text, avoid these options and stick with the regular weight. You want a font that asserts its dominance on the page but still gives you room to add bold for emphasis, if you want. While using light and ultra-light fonts is in vogue for much packaging, it is a terrible choice for text that is intended to be read. While it may look visually appealing, the text is often so faint as to make reading a chore.

When it comes to headings, choose whatever weight works for you.

Font Size

Text is often defined in terms of points—one point is one seventy-second of an inch, so the tallest characters in 12-point text are one-sixth of an inch high.

Many people can read text as small as 8 point. Most people can read 10 point. But while people *can* read this text size, they are both bad choices for the main body text. Instead, make 12 point your default minimum size choice.

For some people, 12 point may look too big. For others, it may seem too small. But on the whole, an average reader will find 12 point comfortable to read. And that's the key point—the text should be comfortable to read. If you require the reader to strain, then you increase the chance that they will stop reading, and if the reader stops reading, then you've lost your chance to influence. Of course, if you think 12 point looks too small, then use something bigger.

Before you start writing, you should know your reader, and if you know that your reader (whether individually or as a collective group) has less than perfect eyesight (for instance, you may be writing for a group of seniors), then consider bumping up the font size to 16 point or maybe 18 point. If the reader needs a larger font, they will appreciate the consideration, and since they won't be spending time looking for a magnifying glass, you will increase your chance of being read.

Font Color and Background Color

Another factor in making your text easy to read is the choice of font color. It's not so much an issue of the absolute choice of color, but more the tonal contrast between the font color and the background color.

If you produce black text on a white background, that will give a good, strong tonal contrast, meaning—all other factors being equal—your text will be easy to read. If, however, you select a light gray background with a slightly lighter gray text, then no matter how big the font and irrespective of the font face, that text will be hard to read.

The difficulty with slightly lighter gray on a light gray background is not simply that both colors are essentially the same—it's a matter that there's no tonal distinction.

If, instead, you chose to replace the font color—perhaps swapping out very light gray for a light powdery blue—thinking that the blue/gray contrast would work, you could still find problems. Tonally light blue and light gray look similar, hence there would be little contrast and the text would still not be readable. A similar challenge is likely to occur with any other tonally light color.

People with sight challenges can often find that light text on a dark background (in other words, white text on a black background) works better than the reverse (the more conventional black on white). The reason is that our retinas adjust to the dominant very light/bright background. For people with sight challenges, once their retinas have adjusted to the bright background, it can then be hard to make out the dark text—this is particularly the case with text on screens.

Clearly you can't always control all of these issues—but if you can, then consider people with sight challenges. And—since you will know your readership—if you have a large proportion of readers who have sight challenges, take some time to understand their specific issues so you can ensure that your text is read.

Line Height and Paragraph Spacing

Line height and line spacing are interchangeable terms. I know layout techs will be screaming that they are two different concepts, but the net effect is the same—they control how much space there is between each line.

And they are important because they affect the readability of text.

If the line spacing is too narrow, then text from adjacent lines will overlap. Beyond the overlap, the closer the lines, the more crowded the text will look. Each paragraph will also appear denser—and it will be denser because there is the same quantity of ink (or electronic equivalent of ink) contained within a smaller area. As you increase the line spacing, the text will appear airier.

There is a practical consideration here. At the end of each line, the reader must move their eyes back to the start of the next line. If the lines are too close, then it is tough for the reader to flick their eyes to the next line—this can lead to lines being re-read and lines being skipped.

If it is hard for the reader to move to the right line *every time*, this is a hint that the line spacing needs to be tweaked and a bit more air added. However, at some point, if you add too much air, then the link from one line to another will be lost.

Generally, a line spacing in the region of 120 percent to 140 percent is acceptable for most people. However, the precise choice is in part dependent upon the font. Some fonts take up more or less vertical space, giving a denser or lighter look on the page (or screen). This perception will have an effect on the readability and therefore on your choice of line spacing.

One other aspect that has an impact on readability is paragraph spacing. Paragraph spacing shows a reader where one paragraph ends and the next begins. This allows the reader to see each separate chunk of information that has been presented by the writer. Without some form of paragraph delineation, the reader is presented with a monolithic chunk of text that can be quite daunting to consume—not to mention the text is much harder to read, even with appropriate line spacing, because line repeating/ skipping will be more likely to occur.

Conventionally, there are two ways to delineate paragraphs.

First, each paragraph can be separated by an empty line. This quite literally gives a space between paragraphs and works well. However, the downside is that it takes up more physical space, which can be an issue if you are producing your document in hard form (in other words, on paper), since each sheet of paper has a finite size, and increasing the space required means you require more paper.

The alternative is to have no break between paragraphs, but to indent the first line of each paragraph: the indent from the left-hand margin then delineates the paragraph break.

Either approach works, and you may want to choose different approaches depending on how the document will be presented.

Line Length

Line length is a factor that is often overlooked. People will take a sheet of paper, set the margins, and what is left is the line length. The result is that readers are presented with lines of text that are too wide—there is too much text, too many characters, on the line.

Excessive line length is a problem because when we read our eyes have trouble following along the line, meaning the reader can lose their place or find their eyes become fatigued. A second issue is that when the reader moves to the next line, with longer line lengths it is much harder to move to the correct line—the reader has a tendency to repeat a line or skip a line.

By contrast, having a line length that is too short tends to upset the rhythm of reading and can lead to excessive hyphenation (or crazy justification with widely spaced words).

So, what is the ideal line length? Well...it depends. Generally anything between sixty and eighty characters per line will be acceptable for most people. And just to be clear, line length is a function of font size—smaller fonts require physically shorter line lengths, and physically longer line lengths are required by larger fonts. Irrespective of the font size, the number of characters per line should be similar.

However, the line length is also a function of line height—as a very, very, very rough rule of thumb, the greater the line height, the longer the line length the reader can tolerate. Of course, there is a limit here—both to line length and to line spacing—but for modest tweaks, look at the two in combination. And when it comes to deciding what is right, you just have to read the text and make a judgment.

If you're still not sure what is ideal, read some newspapers or magazines—there's a reason why these publications adopt columns and generally these print documents are set up with a view to being read.

Pull Quotes, Tint Boxes

Pick up any newspaper or magazine, and you'll see pull quotes, tint boxes, and any number of layout and presentational flourishes intended to make a piece more interesting and to draw the reader in.

The main aim of pull quotes (they're those big quotes you see positioned in the middle of the page, saying something catchy/controversial) is to draw the reader in. Tint boxes (boxes with a different background color) are often used to summarize—for instance, to highlight significant data points or to list key areas.

As tools, these (and the other presentational flourishes) have their use. If you want to use them, use them. However...

While these tools have a use, they are frequently abused and there are other considerations. The main consideration is that these tools are only useful if you have full control over every element of the layout. If you don't, the quote could be misplaced (or not placed), the tint box could be the wrong color, and the data inside the tint box could be presented in a way that distorts the meaning (for instance, a table grid could be lost, leaving some unintelligible numbers).

There's a bigger issue to consider: necessity. While these tools can help, they can also become a crutch. If you need a pull quote to grab interest, then think about the start of the article—the heading, the first paragraph or two. If these haven't grabbed your reader, then even if the quote encourages the reader to start the piece, they'll likely get bored quite soon and stop reading.

But to repeat: used well, these tools can help a reader understand a message.

Lack of Control

If you are producing your work as a printed document—and you are supervising the production—then you can exert a fair degree of control over the end product that will be delivered to your reader.

In these circumstances, you will be able to control the font choice, the line spacing, and the line length, among other factors. In other words, you will be able to optimize the document to make it readable.

However, as soon as you move away from a printed document—where you have supervised the production—then you start to lose control over the output. In some cases you should take action to try to assert your wishes over what the reader will see, and in others you should not make any intervention, because anything you do is likely to be counterproductive and lead to a degraded experience for the reader.

And, in case I need to mention it again, a degraded reading experience usually equates to the writer losing influence.

Let's take a look in more detail.

Printed Documents

I've mentioned that the writer needs to supervise the printing in order to control the end result. Clearly, I'm not suggesting that the writer needs to head off to the printing presses and check each printed copy. However, for any document that is intended to influence, the writer does need to understand the process by which that document will be produced—especially if that process will be different in different locations.

Two factors control the output:

- The format of the file sent to the printer

- What the printer then does with the file

Let's look at these in some more detail.

File Format

There are two main options for how you deliver your file to the printer:

■ Print ready

■ Not print ready

The choice has implications for the output.

PDF format is an example of a print-ready file. The file defines the layout of every page (including the precise positioning of the text), and all of the necessary elements (such as fonts and images) are embedded within the file.

A standard word-processor file is an example of a non-print-ready format. Some word processors do attempt to include print-ready features—for instance, allowing fonts to be embedded—but on the whole, files created with word processors are subject to variation and interpretation, meaning that you cannot control the output.

Much of the difficulty arises with minor changes being made at the printing end of the chain. Typically with word processor files, when the file is opened, fonts may be changed if the exact font is not available on the user's machine. The font may be close, but there may be minor differences, and equally other minor changes may get introduced—for instance, the spacing between each individual character may be changed.

Changing the spacing between each character does not, in and of itself, make a significant change to the look of a document; however, it can have consequential effects. For instance, it can lead to lines breaking in different places, and these line breaks can lead to unexpected page breaks. With different breaks, you can then find that a well-placed pull quote is moved to a position where it is both irrelevant and confusing.

Another change that will occur with word processor files is when they are sent to different countries. If you create an A4 document (which is the standard paper size nearly everywhere but the US) and send the document to the US, typically it will be printed on letter-sized paper (and the converse will be true). Since the page formats are marginally different (A4 is approximately one-quarter of an inch narrower and one-quarter of an inch taller) the printed output will be different.

What the Printer Does with Your File

To be clear, when I talk about the printer, I'm not suggesting that every document will be sent to a commercial printer. If, for instance, you send a report (in a non-print-ready format) to a client and the client prints out that report to distribute internally, then the client is the printer. Equally, if you have prepared a document for the client to print, and the client instead decides to read the document in electronic format, that is still effectively a printing intervention that may subvert your layout intentions.

If you are relying on someone to print the file who is not in the business of being a printer, your ability to influence the output is limited. Even if you send a print-ready file, there is still much scope for change (for instance, the document could be printed on the wrong size paper or the wrong color paper, or its size could be scaled up or down).

If you're using a commercial printer, then the printer will expect you to supply a print-ready file in a format that you have agreed with the printer. As an aside—and way beyond the scope of this book—there are many PDF standards and variants. Simply sending a PDF (or any other print-ready format) won't guarantee the output—it needs to be in a format that the printer understands how to handle.

The advantage of using a commercial printer is that the printer can be expected to use the appropriate paper (right color, right size, right quality, all as specified by you) and the printer will also (usually) not mess around with your file (since the file is print ready).

Electronic Documents: PDFs

When you move your output from print to electronic, you lose much of the control over that layout (for reasons I'll discuss below). Some people try to counter this lack of control by using PDFs.

If your aim is to influence an individual or a small number of individuals, and those individuals are happy to receive your work in PDF form, then this may be a viable option.

If, however, you are posting information more generally—for instance, you are putting out information on the internet or simply sending an email—then don't use PDFs. Seriously, don't. First, you're putting up a barrier (the PDF has to be opened and a special viewer may be needed). Second, you're making the text virtually impossible to wrangle on mobile devices (because the page will have been laid out for one width and the mobile device will likely have a narrower window). Third, some people still find ways to mess with how PDFs are viewed, and force the text to be reflowed.

So, if you're not going to use PDFs, what should you do?

Electronic Documents: Email

Many companies go to great efforts to create highly designed emails. Some of these emails work very well, but many don't.

Every email client has its own special way of mangling emails. As a writer you cannot control the device on which your reader will view an email. This could mean that fonts, layouts, and images are stripped out. Also, many people choose to view emails as plain text.

As a general rule of thumb, if you know the email setup of the individual to whom you are sending your email and you know that the formatting will not be stripped, then consider including formatting in your email. If you don't know or can't be certain about the recipient's email setup, then assume your email will be viewed as plain text and format the text accordingly (so, for instance, put a double return to indicate paragraph breaks and don't bother with a font choice beyond the default).

Electronic Documents: Web Pages

One way you can have a degree of control over the presentation of your text is by posting on a website.

Your Own Website

With your own website, you can fully control all elements of presentation, so, to a certain extent, you can achieve the same control as you can with a printed document where you supervise the printing.

Modern web practices offer great control and flexibility, so you can define the precise fonts and the exact colors, sort the line height and line width, and so on. Modern practice is to have sites adjust the presentation of their content depending on whether it is being viewed on a large screen, a tablet-sized screen, or a phone-sized screen. You can adopt finer-grained control (or simply adopt a practice that works over a wider range of devices).

You can control how your website is set up, but it is harder to control how your website is viewed.

Browsers have numerous plug-ins and add-ons available that are designed to suppress advertisements, tracking beacons, and many other web elements. This often leads to the layout and presentation of a website being altered. Equally, some web browsers (particularly older browsers) do not adhere to web standards and are simply incapable of correctly rendering a web page.

Whether elements on your web page are blocked as a matter of choice or are forced on your reader by their browser, you should plan for any web page to have some or all of its presentation features blocked. And when planning for how your web page could be mangled at the reader's end, as a first step don't try to be too clever with your presentation—don't try to use the latest and greatest techniques.

Seriously, it's the argument you're making that matters, not the presentation—the web equivalent of bright flashing lights doesn't help the reader better understand, nor does it increase your influence. Question every step you make beyond presenting plain text to your reader. People have been reading black text on white(ish) paper for years—it seems to have worked well, so why change?

Second, have a fallback position. In designing web pages, it is conventional to have fallback font choices—so, if font A isn't available, the text will be rendered with font B, and if font B isn't available.... But take this further. Look at every element of presentation and assume it will be stripped out, then review what you have left. If what you have left does not convey the influence you are intending, then fix the text. Don't fix the web page—fix the text.

Third-Party Websites

You may be presenting your arguments on a website that you don't control—this could include a news/magazine website or one of the blogging websites.

If you cannot control the presentation—for instance, you have no influence over the choice of font, the line height, and the line length—then clearly there's no gain to trying to change what you cannot change. You have to live with what you've got.

However, what you can do is understand how your words will be presented. Take some time to preview how your text will look when it is presented by the website, and if any element makes the reader's task less than easy, consider changes to your text to accommodate.

The options open to you will be limited, but you can make tweaks. For instance, shorter paragraphs may address problems with line height/line length, and using lists (whether numbered or bulleted) may help the reader focus on key points you want to draw out.

Electronic Documents: eBooks

eBooks are, in essence, web pages. Crack open the file, and an ebook is a collection of web pages, some images, maybe some fonts, layout instructions, and don't forget an index—all bundled into a single file that can be readily distributed.

Where web pages are viewed through a browser, ebooks are read with specialized reading devices. These devices may be dedicated hardware devices—such as the Kindle—or ebook apps for tablets and phones (for example, the Kindle app and the iBooks app).

And as you might expect, since the root of ebooks is the web page, there are a range of presentation options and a number of presentation challenges.

While there are options—and you definitely should think about how you present ebooks—don't try too hard. All you will end up doing is fighting with the reader's preferences and fighting with the device overrides. The net result will be wasted time on your part and an unhappy reader. Oh yeah, and that influence thing...

The approaches for paper documents and electronic documents designed to be read on a specialized reading device are different. With paper, if you don't make a decision, then the page remains blank. With paper, once printed, the page is fixed—the only person who can influence how the material is presented to the reader is you. By contrast, with a reading device, the reader will set their own font, line height, and line length. They will choose settings that they find appealing and that make it comfortable for them to read.

You do not know better than your reader. Trying to impose your views about presentation and layout on a reader—when the reader can control those issues—is not a good use of your time.

However, as I said, this doesn't mean you should do nothing. Instead, you should be thinking about the fallback position and helping the reader to understand and interpret the text. Maybe I can best illustrate these issues by looking at some of the choices I specified for the electronic version of this book.

Fonts

For the electronic version of this book, I have not specified a default body font but I have set the default heading font to sans serif. In other words, I have only suggested the fallback fonts for the heading and the user specified font (or default font for the device) will be selected for the body text.

eBooks offer the opportunity to embed fonts. Superficially this can seem like a good idea. In practice it is a terrible notion. First, you're imposing your will on the reader when they've almost certainly already set their own preference. Second, you cannot know how a font will render. It may look good on your screen, but you cannot know how it will look for the reader. What might be crisp and clear for you may become a blurry mess for the reader.

Font Size

The body text for the electronic version of this book has been set to 100 percent. In other words, I have specified no adjustment—the font *should* appear to be the same size as the body text in any book the reader reads. I have made no point-size specification (so, for instance, I haven't specified the body text should be 12 point). The reason for not specifying a point size is that I cannot know whether the reader is using any zoom/magnification function.

I specified the headings to be larger—headings are larger than subheadings, and subheadings are larger than sub-subheadings. In all cases, the heading size has been set as a percentage, so if the body text size is increased or decreased, then the heading size should be increased or decreased correspondingly. I say *should* because I cannot know how the ebook will render on every reading device.

Line Height

I have set a default line height. As with the font size, my default line height has been set as a percentage (rather than an absolute point setting) so that it retains its effect when the text is increased or decreased.

Paragraph Spacing

For the electronic version of this book, I haven't set paragraph spacing, but instead I specify an indent for the first line of each paragraph (apart from the first paragraph for each chapter).

The reason I don't bother with setting the spacing after paragraphs is that while I like the look and believe it aids reader comprehension, many (perhaps most) electronic reading devices simply ignore any paragraph spacing setting. Virtually all devices appear to implement the line indent setting, so I use this setting. It may be that in a few years paragraph spacing will be more widely implemented, but until then I'll stick with line indents.

Getting Too Clever

There are ways around some of the challenges posed by electronic reading devices. These are usually ugly kludges, and I recommend you avoid them wherever possible.

I recommend the avoidance first because they are kludges, and second because you're putting yourself at the mercy of your reader's device software. If an app is updated, then it could easily "fix" the kludge upon which you are relying, thereby turning your finely tuned output into a horrid mess.

Screen Readers

Screen readers take text—usually on a computer screen—and convert that text to speech or in some cases to braille. This software is typically used by the visually impaired.

Screen readers typically start reading from the top of the page and follow the text as written. Placing a pull quote or a tint box in the middle of the page may invite a sighted reader to read the article, but for a visually challenged reader these flourishes can be confusing, not least because they can be inserted into the middle of sentences.

The more layout flourishes you implement, the more you will likely find that some of your readers are affected.

Form versus Function

It's easy to ignore form and focus exclusively on function. It's easy to see the two as being exclusive. In truth, there is a continuum, and one influences the other.

In the case of the written word, both the attractiveness of the presentation and the practicality of reading the text have a major impact on how well you can exert your influence.

The good news is that sorting the appearance of your text is much easier than getting the words themselves right.

Chapter 7

Cut and Simplify: Editing

O nce you have written, then it's time to edit. But what do we mean when we talk about editing, and what should we expect from the process?

What Is Editing?

Editing is where the hard work really starts. There are two main aims in editing:

- To improve what has been written. For the editor to identify areas where you, the writer, may want to consider changes that—in the editor's opinion—will improve the piece.

- To remove errors and problematic material. This can be anything from typographical errors, through constantly shifting voice and tense, past weak and confusing arguments, up to and including unintended offense.

There are several aspects to an edit—different areas where you can look for improvement and to remove problems—but the main areas of focus are:

- Spelling, grammar, punctuation, and technical aspects of writing.

- Accuracy in terms of what you are putting forward—are your facts actually facts, and are those facts supported by evidence?

- Are the advice and influence correct, coherent, and relevant to the reader?

We'll look at each aspect in more detail.

Do I Need an Edit?

But do I need an edit? I mean, do I really, really, really need an edit?

There is never an occasion when writing will not benefit from an edit. Never. But I'm an expert, I hear someone mutter—I know more than anyone! What could an editor add? If you're making these sorts of claims, then you're blind to the possibility of error or improvement—and if you're blind to these possibilities, then you're no expert and you've just proved why an edit is so important.

No one gets anything right first time. No one. If you think you do, you're a fool.

Your edit is the opportunity to refine your writing. Typically when we write, we have too much information in our head, which we can't write down quickly enough. Editing allows us that second chance to really say what we meant to say in the first place. Equally, we miss things and make mistakes. All problems can be fixed in an edit.

Scope of the Edit

While an edit is fundamental, there are some more significant questions to address before we jump in:

- Who should undertake the edit?

- What scope should the edit encompass?

The identity of the editor may not be a single person. In many instances, it will be appropriate to have a range of editors, each with their own specialties. Clearly, the range of people involved will then, to a certain extent, answer the secondary question about the scope of the edit (or more likely, a decision about the scope of the edit will drive the decision about who is the right person, or the right people, to undertake the work).

If you are to involve anyone beyond yourself in the editing process, then those other people should be bringing something to the party. Involving other people is not about making them feel good—it is about improving the final written product. It is about involving different people with different skills and different perspectives so that you—the writer—get a wider view on your piece.

And the involvement of other people should most definitely not lead to writing by committee, where the final output is simply a compromise between competing views. If you can't decide a singular view, then you will fail at influence. If you can't decide a singular view, then the problem is not with your writing—it's with the underlying issue around which you are trying to influence.

Who Should Edit?

The question of who should edit is always a thorny one, and I hope it's clear that I'm in favor of bringing an external perspective. However, as I have alluded, there are times when a self-edit may be appropriate.

It's important to understand that a self-edit is just that. It is an edit undertaken by the writer. The editing process laid out in this chapter should be followed in the same manner—it is just undertaken by the writer.

In no way should a self-edit become no edit or a bad edit.

And as an aside, as a simple matter of courtesy, every document should be self-edited before it is passed to other editors.

If the writing is short and the risks/stakes associated with the influence are low, then self-editing can be appropriate.

But for longer documents and especially where the risks/ stakes are elevated, remove your ego from the equation and find someone to bring a new perspective to what you have written.

Never-Ending Edit

An edit is not a scientific process or checklist. Instead, it is an activity carried out by human beings, looking at the work of other human beings. As you might expect with these parameters, there will be mistakes, and the final output will never be perfect.

If you think your writing has been edited, past tense, you're wrong. It can always be edited some more. Always.

However, as the writer, you need to call time and at a certain point accept that what you have written is *good enough*.

Elements of an Edit

An edit is not a singular thing—there are many aspects and views to be considered.

Copy Edit

What is often called a copy edit is, in essence, a review of the technical aspects of writing. Simply put, it is a check that all the words are spelled correctly and that commas and other punctuation marks are in the right place.

But there is much more to the line edit. It's a basic—and yet fundamental—check of each sentence and each paragraph. The editor will ask themselves, Does this make sense? Does this say what the writer is intending to say?

So, what should you focus on and what can you expect from a line edit?

Spelling

Spelling is always a challenge. It is a challenge first because language develops, and as a consequence, spellings change. Second, it's a challenge because there are variants of English with different spellings. English, as in the language spoken by the English, and American English, to give two examples, have many different and subtle spelling variants. That said, there are many variant spellings within British English; for instance, many words can be spelled with either an S or a Z (as an example, energise and energize are both correct British English spellings).

Fundamentally, spelling doesn't matter. What matters is what your reader understands. You can spell words in any manner that makes you happy, but if you spell them in a way that your reader can't immediately understand the word, then you will have lost influence. You should also remember that if you spell in an unconventional manner, your reader may think you simply can't spell, and if the reader has this attitude, then they're likely to question everything you write.

Whatever your spelling choice, remain consistent. So if you choose energize, then stick with energize—don't occasionally use energise.

British English

One quick word for the Brits—and here, in case there's any doubt, I write as a British subject.

Culturally, we won. Our language is the most widely spoken language around the globe. But it's not the most widely written language, and as I mentioned earlier, language is always in flux.

American English is the most widely written and most widely understood. It is also the direction in which British English is moving. Maybe slowly, but one autocorrect at a time, British English is becoming more Americanized.

My advice to my fellow Brits—and to the citizens of the Commonwealth who speak and write a more British-infused version of English—is to adopt American English as far as makes sense. If there's a question about spelling (color or colour, for instance), then choose the American variant.

Choose the American variant because it will be more widely understood. Choose the American variant because British English readers understand American English more than the converse. Choose American English so your writing doesn't become dated as American English becomes more accepted in the British English world.

There will be times when you feel an overwhelming need to choose British English words—and in that case, go ahead and choose the British English—but use the American English spelling (if there is a difference). Equally, be alert to American English terms that are coming the other way—for instance, the British English concept of a text message sent from your mobile phone is more widely understood than the now somewhat archaic earlier American version of an SMS message sent from a cell phone.

Punctuation

You will have already read my suggestion to avoid punctuation as far as possible. The editing process provides the opportunity to strip out any unnecessary punctuation that has slipped through.

Readers have difficulty understanding what is meant by punctuation...which is not surprising, since many writers don't quite understand what they're doing with punctuation. Readers clearly understand full stops, but beyond that, it gets tough.

If the meaning of what you have written is changed or can be interpreted differently depending on the presence (or lack of presence) of any punctuation marks, then there is a problem with the matter you are trying to express. Do not look to repunctuate—or expect your editor to fix the problem with a few punctuation tweaks. There is no magic here. Simply rewrite what you are intending to say in a clearer manner. Clearer will usually mean shorter sentences with a more straightforward word choice.

Punctuation and Abbreviations

There are many rules around punctuation and abbreviation. But there's also a lot of superstition and much misunderstanding. There's also a difference in practice between British English and American English.

With this confusion, if you want to plow your own furrow, please do. But, as I've said before, whatever choice you make, be consistent.

With American English, the conventional practice is to insert a period to indicate where a word has been shortened, thus Doctor becomes Dr. and Mister becomes Mr.

In British English, the conventional practice is not to include a full stop, so United Kingdom becomes UK, Doctor becomes Dr, and Mister becomes Mr without any trailing punctuation.

If you're writing British English, never include any full stops in connection with abbreviations. If you're writing American English and you're in any doubt about whether to include periods, drop them. Even if you're not in doubt, give serious consideration to dropping periods. With this approach, you run the risk that some American readers may think that there's a typographical error, but in my opinion, that risk is not that significant.

The reason to drop the use of periods is that the tide is flowing against the practice. The rules are already blurred with the use of acronyms (where periods are less frequently employed), and with the use of mobile devices, typing periods is tiresome and leads to autocorrect errors (for instance, the automatic insertion of spaces after periods).

And also stop it, because inserting periods just looks plain ugly.

Spaces After a Full Stop

One area where people seem to get really bent out of shape is with the number of spaces after a full stop. There are historical reasons here, but they are irrelevant.

The short answer to this question is to put one space after a full stop.

The longer answer is, Who cares? Do whatever you want—just be consistent. Seriously, you're not going to go to writers' jail because you chose two spaces after a full stop.

Self-Copy Editing

There are several challenges with self-copy editing, not least that we see what we intended to write, rather than what is actually written, and we have a tendency to skip over material we *feel* is right.

While not scientific, there are few actions the self-copy editor can take to bring out errors:

- Read the material aloud. Somehow this makes errors jump out and gives an indication of when material literally doesn't sound right.

- Put the material into a different format. For instance, print it out or view it on a different device. The different appearance will help you see the document in a new light.

- Change the font/font size—this is another variant on making the document look different. Make the change and read the document, then revert to the appropriate font before publication.

- Read the document backward. You'll lose all sense of meaning, but it is one way of helping odd words to jump out.

Line Edit

The line between a line edit and a copy edit is fine, and indeed the two roles can overlap or be covered by one person.

The intent behind a line edit is to look at the content and to help the writer knock the text into best possible shape.

What Is Important?

The line editor will look to understand what is important. If everything is important, then nothing is important.

Nuances and intricacies need to be highlighted. But equally, nuances and intricacies are often second-order issues that should not detract from the main area of influence.

Areas where you cannot reach a conclusion should be highlighted. It's perfectly acceptable not to have knowledge in a certain area, but you need to be honest and not imply to the reader that you know but you're not saying. Equally, if there is an area where you lack knowledge, that lack of knowledge should not be the focus—the focus should be the issue around which you are attempting to influence.

The line editor can provide a dispassionate view about how well you have focused your document.

Simplify, Simplify, Simplify

Through the edit, you should always look to ways to simplify what you are saying. The intent here should not be to simplify your content, but to simplify how you communicate. Can you find a better word or phrase—one that more clearly expresses what you want to express? Can you remove any confusion or contradiction that might cause the reader to hesitate or misunderstand your point?

In short, can you make the words better? Can you say what you want to say in fewer words?

Ugly, Ugly Words and Phrases

Your copy editor will take out some ugly words and phrases. Hopefully your line editor will kill the rest.

So, what are these ugly words? Well, they take many forms. Here are few examples:

- Words and phrases that have no meaning. For instance, "going forward." Well, if we're talking about future planning, you can't go backward.

- Verbosity. For instance, "Would you please be so good as to..." Far simpler to say: "Please..."

- Redundancy. For instance, "Let me be clear: I disagree." If you need to add "Let me be clear" in order to express your disagreement, then you have failed in your writing.

- Pomposity, such as "With reference to yours of the 15th inst."

There are many other examples. You'll recognize them if you look.

Humor

If any humor has snuck through, squash it. Humor is generally a good thing, but it's bad in writing.

And it's bad for any number of reasons, especially that humor is highly subjective and there's a good chance that much of your audience will not get the humor. It also ages badly.

So, take out humor and take out sarcasm.

There's another significant reason to avoid humor. Humor is about entertainment, and we're aiming for influence.

Equally, if there are any other elements of entertainment, they should be removed. We're not writing as a journalist with an audience who expects their schtick. We're writing for influence; therefore, the focus should be on the influence.

Editing Paragraphs

For every sentence and paragraph, the question should be asked: Would it detrimentally affect the reader's understanding if this sentence/paragraph were deleted? If the understanding would not be detrimentally affected, then the sentence or paragraph should be removed.

And if the sentence or paragraph cannot be removed, then it must be important. If it's important, then why doesn't it come earlier in the piece?

Depending on the length of the piece, as I've already mentioned, it's often good to read it out loud. This is a great check to hear whether the writing literally sounds right. Also, it's a great way to check sentence length—if a sentence cannot be spoken in one breath (without straining), then it is probably too long and/or may be too convoluted with too many subclauses, parenthetical thoughts, and the like.

Factual Edit

A factual edit—sometimes called a technical edit—is very different from a line edit or a copy edit. The aim is not to correct spellings, find grammatical errors, or look at whether the piece is well written. Instead a factual edit has one aim: to ensure what is written is technically correct. This is about accuracy in terms of what you are putting forward—are your facts actually facts, and are those facts supported by evidence?

The factual edit requires very different skills from a copy edit or a line edit. The factual editor does not need an understanding of grammar and spelling—they need a full and detailed knowledge of the subject that is being written about. In other words, the identity of the factual editor will be driven by the content that needs to be reviewed.

A factual edit is always necessary. Always.

Other imperatives (such as money and time) may drive the choice of factual editor, but it will always be beneficial for the factual edit to be undertaken by someone other than the writer.

The skills of the copy/line editor are different from those required for a factual editor, but that doesn't mean there can't be a skills overlap. There is nothing to stop the line/copy editor from undertaking the factual edit if they have the knowledge. There is often benefit in having another voice, but again, time and cost will likely influence decisions.

Advice/Influence Edit

The final editing perspective is to look at the advice and influence of the piece.

Beyond getting the spelling and commas right, beyond the facts, there is another issue—whether the conclusion drawn by the piece is right for the reader. Every fact may be totally correct, but if you have laid them out and drawn a conclusion that is just plain wrong for the reader, then your influence will fail.

The advice/influence edit will also look at coherence and relevance. The editor will ask whether the totality of the piece is coherent and the totality of the piece is relevant for the reader.

Proofreading

The final step before you publish (or hit the send button) is to proofread. As with the edits, this is best done by someone other than the writer—fresh eyes can spot any number of mistakes.

The purpose of proofreading is to make one last check. The proofreader should not be suggesting new or different material. If the proofreader does suggest changes, that would highlight a failure of the editing process (whether in the choice of editors or in the quality of work they undertook, or maybe a failure by the author to implement reasonable changes).

The proofreader should not be the writer. However, if you are proofing your own work, then leave as much time as possible before you proofread. Ideally, you want to leave the document overnight—or better, over a weekend—before you return for your final read. Clearly, this sort of delay may not always be practical, but the longer you can leave, the fresher the document will seem when you read it, and the more likely you will be to find errors.

Keep on Editing

Editing is not a simple one-step event. It is a continuous process.

The edit is important. It is the process where you can immeasurably improve the quality of your output, and it is also the place where you can get lost with many competing voices and a clamor for absolute perfection.

Throughout the process, you need to remain guided by two central principles:

- Who are you trying to influence?

- What are you asking of them?

Keep your focus on those two aspects, and your edit will be straightforward.

Chapter 8

To Conclude

I'd love to be able to conclude this book with *one thing*. But in truth, to write for influence requires bringing together many, many elements and aligning every element to point in the right direction. There are many ways to be wrong but far fewer to be right, and the wrongs can have disproportionate effect on your influence because they can stop the reader reading.

That said, there are some fundamentals.

Fundamentals

- Focus on the reader.

- Write short sentences and short (less than one hundred words) paragraphs.

- Each paragraph should contain a single thought and no more.

- Use the fewest words possible, but make what you say relevant. People can reread something that's good, but if it's long and dull they won't read anything.

- The writer and the writer's credentials are irrelevant. All that matters is the benefit for the reader.

- Influence takes time.

- If you don't have communication, you can't influence.

- The need to communicate means you might not be able to get to where you want to go immediately. The reality is that moving people takes time, and you need to go slowly. This slowness may be frustrating, but it is better to move in small steps than not to move at all (or worse, to go backward because you anti-influence).

- And if you can't be interesting, be brief. Please. Be as brief as you can in any event, but if you're going to be dull—especially if you're going to impose your "style"—then be really brief.

But?

For much of this book, I've essentially said don't take that course, take this one instead, and I'm sure you often have mentally asked, Can't I do both?

No.

The point here is focus. If you want to influence, then influence. If you want to entertain, then go ahead and entertain, but remember, your influence will be diluted and lost.

There's one question: what matters most? Either influence matters or something else—pick one and only one. If you don't choose influence and commit to influence, then don't be surprised if you fail to influence.

Enough

That's it. Put down the book and get writing.

About the Author

Simon Cann is the author of the Boniface, Leathan Wilkey, and Montbretia Armstrong novels.

In addition to his fiction, Simon has written a range of audio-related and business-related books, including the *How to Make a Noise* series, the most widely read series about synthesizer sound programming, and *Made it in China*, about entrepreneurs building businesses in China. He has also worked as a ghostwriter.

Before turning full-time to writing, Simon worked as a management consultant, where his clients included aeronautical, pharmaceutical, defense, financial services, chemical, entertainment, and broadcasting companies.

He lives in London.

If you've got something to say about how we communicate, or you want to hear more, then come and join the conversation with Simon at the Words We Choose To Use website (wordswechoosetouse.com).